To Alek
with best regards,

Mike Marriott
Nov 2001

Praise for *Power Play*

Industries are being revolutionized by the effects of the digital economy. In today's fast-paced environment, the commonsense approach to organizational success is often obscured by unrealistic visions and quick fixes. *Power Play* avoids the short-term thinking prevalent in recent years, and focuses instead on developing a lasting solution for beating the competition.

—*Bob Rudzki, Senior Vice President, Bayer Corporation*

Moriarty and Klassen have clearly demonstrated the efficiency and service-level benefits of net markets. Using the concepts and lessons of this book will help any business harness the power of these markets.

—*Doug Stone, Senior Vice President, Qwest*

Power Play cuts to the chase of the Internet's potential. Net marketplaces will change the way the biggest companies do business. Thanks to Moriarty and Klassen for shining a light on this unfolding revolution.

—*Phillip Merrick, Chairman and CEO, webMethods*

Power Play provides the insights and guidance necessary to compete successfully in Internet markets . . . a must read for any company looking to gain a competitive edge.

—*Jeff Smith, Vice President/GM, Commerce One Ventures*

The past year has been a proving ground for lessons in net markets. *Power Play* synthesizes these lessons and provides valuable insights for executives in all industries who are committed, anxious or just plain intrigued about the possibilities of "e."

—*Bob Lewis, Chief Executive Officer, Converge*

A year ago, the pendulum swung in favor of everything "e." Now, a year later, it has swung firmly in the opposite direction. As the authors demonstrate, neither extreme is accurate. The power of net markets is neither a cure-all nor a downfall, but a tool for improving the bottom line.
—Keith Melbourne, General Manager,
Trading Community Business Unit, Hewlett-Packard

The bottom line is sustainable value. In this book, Moriarty and Klassen describe the characteristics that will divide the many electronic marketplaces now on the web into the few winners...and the many losers. An insightful read for entrepreneurs and VCs focused in this area.
—Tim Connors, Partner, Sequoia Capital

Net markets are corporate "cyber bazaars"; very personal and efficient when correctly conceived and implemented. *Power Play* provides a template to help understand what to look for when assessing the impact of net markets on your corporation.
—Tim Guleri, General Partner, Sierra Ventures

The secrets to achieving sustainable growth are easy to understand in concept...but difficult to achieve in practice. Our colleagues Mike Moriarty and Bruce Klassen are onto something with this new book. They know that there are no easy wins in the digital marketplace, and that only those organizations that position themselves for growth and which invest for the long term will be able to capture the value promised by the new economy.
—Fritz Kroeger and James McGrath,
coauthors, The Value Growers

POWER PLAY

The Beginning of the Endgame in Net Markets

MIKE MORIARTY
BRUCE KLASSEN

John Wiley & Sons, Inc.

New York • Chichester • Weinheim • Brisbane • Singapore • Toronto

Published by John Wiley & Sons, Inc.
Published simultaneously in Canada.

This publication is designed to provide accurate and authoritative information in regard to the subject matter covered. It is sold with the understanding that the publisher is not engaged in rendering professional services. If professional advice or other expert assistance is required, the services of a competent professional person should be sought.

Library of Congress Cataloging-in-Publication Data

Moriarty, Mike.
    Power play : the beginning of the endgame in Net markets / Michael Moriarty, Bruce N. Klassen.
        p. cm.
    Includes bibliographical references and index.
    ISBN 0-471-43880-4 (cloth : alk. paper)
    1. Electronic commerce. 2. Business enterprises—Computer networks.
  3. Internet I. Klassen, Bruce N. II. Title.

HF5548.32 .M67 2001
658.8′4—dc21   2001026444
Printed in the United States of America.

10 9 8 7 6 5 4 3 2 1

With love to Joan,
who makes it all worthwhile,
And to Nicole and Elana,
who will make it all come true.

Contents

Acknowledgments

To collect the best, most up-to-date insights about e-marketplaces, we reached out to those A.T. Kearney colleagues who are actively involved in developing strategy and infrastructure for industry and private exchanges. "May we talk to your clients and ask them what works in your exchange and what needs to be done better?" we asked. Across both oceans, our colleagues graciously replied in the affirmative. We can never repay the willingness expressed by Sid Abrams, Peter Appel, Toby Kilgore, Vas Kodali, Bernhard Rieder, Andy Schmidt, and Christoph Wiese. Thank you.

They weren't the only colleagues whose collective wisdom we tapped, repeatedly. The list of content contributors includes Chris Ahn, Jonathan Anscombe, Johan Aurik, Danny Chaturvedi, Richard Coffey, Sheila Crowther, John Cruse, Larry Guevel, Omar Hijazi, Gillis Jonk, Philipp Jung, Dave Skeels, Ben Smith, and Bob Willen. They not only allowed us to interview them for their expert net marketing knowledge; they formed a panel of experts to review the content and ensure that the manuscript reflected their best knowledge. Thank you.

We also thank the many executives who shared their insights and helped to make this book real-time and practical. They are credited with their quotes in the text. Thank you.

Our research team kept the data updated as dot coms disappeared and alliances came unglued. Stephen Bugman Jr., Brad Bullington, Micah Chamberlain, Melissa Gudell, Deven Patodia, Paul R. Solans, Paul Somerset, Tom Stroud, Kathryn Weismantel, and Jeff Yuille all spent countless hours ensuring that our facts are current. Thank you.

Thank you to the editorial team of Tony Vlamis, Bethany Crawford, and Patricia Sibo. Thank you also to Lee Anne Petry, who was a member of that team and kept our collective eyes on the clock. Special thanks and 10,000 options in the next (genuinely!) big thing go to Martha Peak, who managed the development of this manuscript through 12 of the most tumultuous months the net markets have ever seen and who kept us on-task, on-target, and on-time. Thank you, Marty.

For all that is good and true in this book, we credit these, our hardworking colleagues. For all omissions and errors, we acknowledge responsibility.

POWER
PLAY

Introduction

One must wait until the evening
To see how splendid the day has been
                                        —Sophocles

The executives in the room were talking intently, oblivious to their Parisian surroundings. Meeting just a few weeks after the WorldWide Retail Exchange had conducted its first online auction last year, they were critiquing what went right and what could be done better next time. The auction had been a simple pilot MRO (maintenance, repair, and operations) purchase, but for most firms involved, it was the first time they had come together to the table with archrivals—Power Players all—not to compete, but to work together for the shared goal of saving everyone money. The passion they displayed suggested that this was far from business as usual.

To an onlooker, the meeting was the kind that could make antitrust lawyers flinch. After all, gathered together were senior executives of a score of global retail firms, complete with competitive product lines and overlapping customer bases. And they had come together for a common cause: to find ways to collectively cut costs throughout the industry.

Welcome to the brave new economy. It's a world of net markets, where longtime competitors are now also collaborators. And, because most players wear multiple and morphing hats, they are frequently one another's clients and suppliers as well.

■ GETTING HERE FROM THERE

At first, it didn't seem that this was how e-business would develop. After all, way back in the heady days of 1999 and early 2000, the start-ups were hailed as the winners. Aggressive, agile, entrepreneurial whiz kids thought up innovative marketing schemes and created a new, digital economy that turned them into Wall Street darlings. They turned just about all the conventional wisdom they had learned in business school upside down. They created phenomenal market value—on paper, at least—out of nothing but gutsy business plans with Roman-candle-like revenue forecasts and no profit projections. It seemed like these entrepreneurs were constantly defying gravity.

But as Abraham Lincoln remarked when the Industrial Revolution was still young, you can't fool all the people all of the time. In retrospect, round one didn't last very long. By April 2000, Wall Street stopped waiting for marketing schemes to turn into sustainable new business models, and the bottom fell out of the Nasdaq.

Now, the Power Players are back in the lead position. The men and women of the Fortune 500—and their peers around the globe—have slowly and confidently walked into the ring and joined the e-business fray, bringing all the muscle and deep pockets needed to create and deliver a round-two knockout punch. Incumbent companies have years of know-how about making alliances work, which is a critical and delicate skill in the digital economy. And their deep experience in developing new product lines, in going global, in integrating supply chains, and in wooing customers in sustainable ways are skills that are still critical, even in the new economy.

But although the Power Players lost round one, they picked up some valuable lessons from their upstart competitors. They learned that they need to find new ways to do business in a world that is decidedly different, they learned that they need to do it faster, and they learned that it won't be easy. These are, after all, firms with a great deal invested in the status quo—legacy systems, complex decision-making processes—and with a strong aversion to risk.

■ NO MAGIC POTION

Despite what you may have read in the business pages, e-business never was a magic bullet or a one-size-fits-all fix to old-economy competitive issues. "E" is just an enabler, albeit one of profound importance. As such, "e" has created the links that are allowing incumbent companies in every industry sector to create business-to-business (B2B) market-places that are streamlining the supply chain, improving delivery cycles, and enhancing collaboration. Ultimately, these companies are creating sustainable value that can be passed along to consumers, as well as shared among every-one else along the value chain. And these links are really no more than utilities.

Enter net markets. Announcements of new Internet marketplaces, as well as initial public offerings (IPOs) of existing ones, became everyday occurrences early in 2000. Even for rust-belt products such as steel or chemicals, which are the last thing you think of when you think of "e," a mul-titude of e-marketplaces quickly arose. But that was then. Since the Nasdaq cratered, B2B Internet company stock prices have come back to realistic valuations, and inevitably, so-called web marketplaces are consolidating and disap-pearing. Now, every week seems to bring a spate of layoffs and closures. The steady flow of IPO announcements have been replaced by announcements of postponements due to unfriendly market conditions and by stories of layoffs, even from companies that previously earned headlines for being backed by Wall Street nobility. Given this riotous environ-ment, it seems that unpredictability is the only predictable characteristic of net markets.

Despite the uncertainty, two critical reasons remain fixed that explain why Power Player companies, like yours, need to join (or create their own) net markets now. First, a strong business case for Internet marketplaces results from a comparison between transaction costs using current proprietary technologies and the anticipated costs of using Internet-based data transmission and management technologies. The first examples of reduced costs came when companies realized that they could reduce the request-for-information and request-for-quote (RFI and RFQ, or collectively RFx) processes from weeks to days or hours; the impact on buyer productivity was enormous, and the ability to increase strategic focus was stunning. The Power Players were hooked. When they realized that this same efficiency, with corresponding improvements in effectiveness, could be gained in logistics, import and export, product development, category management, and customer relationship management—well, Goliath got back up and started running after a fleeing David.

The second reason to participate in net markets is that there is no doubt that the *value* inherent in the value chain will be distributed differently in the future. Net markets allow companies to consolidate purchase volumes with either, for example, their own 37 divisions or with 37 of their most formidable competitors. As such, net markets have a dramatic impact on the balance of power of the relationships in today's value chain. One reason the WorldWide Retail Exchange members got together is that, together, these retailers, currently numbering 53, are "bigger than Wal-Mart," with their $750 billion of turnover versus Wal-Mart's mere $190 billion.

In this environment, the development of net markets—even given the ups and downs—is unstoppable. Companies have little choice but to either join an existing market or, for the more adventurous, start their own. Doing nothing, and thus allowing a competitor to drive the change in an industry sector, will dramatically affect a company's competitive standing. And for third parties, net markets have opened an opportunity to step in among sellers and buyers, and to provide the infrastructure to compete in the new environment, in exchange for a percentage of the benefits.

Why should your company help create an e-market or participate in one? Most benefits of net market participation fall into one of these categories:

➤ *Better market information.* The most basic benefit that net markets offer their members is market intelligence. For example, the Internet makes pricing information increasingly transparent and widespread; buyers can search for lower-priced products. Building on this, it's possible to exchange information on specifications, facilitating the search for a better product or service fit.

➤ *Reduced purchase prices.* Net markets also increase transparency between suppliers and buyers by increasing standardization of product specifications. Buyers more easily identify the lowest-priced or highest-quality products by comparison shopping across multiple suppliers. Buyers also pool their purchasing power through a net market to create a single contract, or frame agreement, that serves multiple companies. By pooling demand, they achieve the economies of scale needed to allow suppliers to cut costs out of their value chain. Developing frame agreements is the first step to a real Internet exchange, in which multiple buyers and multiple sellers collectively agree to a buy/sell arrangement that dynamically changes (enabled by Internet technology, of course!) over time and in response to changing market conditions. These frame agreements are the protocols by which all parties define the process of doing business together.

➤ *Improved transactional efficiencies.* All companies maintain multiple order flows; even some barbershops are utilizing new technologies. Orders placed through the phones, fax, web site, or a broker agent who runs around picking up paper orders all cost more—and all these costs are passed along to the consumer.

The promise of e-procurement is no-paper, no-delay, no-sticky-note-on-the-monitor, unified, and conflict-free transaction processing. Improving transactional efficiencies is an important part of what leading companies such as Oracle, Commerce One, and Ariba are doing, as well as emerging companies such as Metreo and Arzoon. The so-called human errors made when placing an order plummet to zero. Consequently, when a supplier's cost to service its customers drops, the resulting savings can be passed on to the end user.

To be perfectly frank, though, many companies rely on the 5 or 8 percent of human-error costs for their profit margin. Think seriously about how it will feel in the future when each negotiation doesn't start with, "Ah, but that's not what I understood...." and the expectation that you will receive some accommodation. If you think this doesn't happen in your company or if you don't think its elimination will be a big cultural change, you should spend more time in your call centers and buyers' offices and then come back and reread this book.

➤ *Reduced inventory levels.* Because net markets permit greater discipline in procurement and in supply chain and category management, companies gain greater control over inventory levels. Remember how your management sciences professor always said that inventory is what you get when you don't know what you'll get? Net markets help you to know what you are going to get, so they help you to avoid inventories. Information replaces physical product. Just-in-time inventory is replaced by just-in-time production, which in turn is replaced by just-in-time materials-requirements planning, which in turn is replaced by ... well, you get the idea. Pretty soon, beans in Argentina aren't sprouting because Mrs. MacGillicuddy in Des Moines decided not to buy Green Giant today.

➤ *Improved service.* When you use an online exchange, supply signals and demand signals collapse in time, and the mystery and uncertainty of the transaction disappears. At a recent supplier summit in Tokyo for one of the leading Internet utilities, interested suppliers were taken through a day-in-the-life demonstration of a product suite that changes the buyer's day from one of launching hopeful proposals into the darkness to one of confirming solutions with full visibility on both sides. With more than three hundred leading suppliers in the hall, the silence was palpable. Given the transparency that net markets can provide to new product design and development efforts, it is no wonder that many executives approach the entire topic with a grave visage or a thoughtful mien. They simply don't know how they are going to change enough, quickly enough.

The potential benefits, the perceived first-mover advantages, and the influence of third parties have resulted in a tremendous rush toward e-marketplaces. They have also led to a no-holds-barred, trial-and-error approach for getting in the game—an approach that has already found some dot-com B2Bs in bankruptcy and will result in more entertaining press coverage of others before the market completes its sweeping market recapitalization.

■ GETTING IN THE GAME

According to A.T. Kearney analysis, by the end of 2001, at least 1,250 exchanges will have been launched, and together they will account for $150 billion in trade. Among them will be the handful of global B2B net markets that will set the pace in their industries. These include the WorldWide Retail Exchange, the global retail sector exchange; Covisint, a landmark venture that was founded by the Big Three automakers—General Motors (GM), DaimlerChrysler, and Ford—and which quickly went global by signing up Renault and Nissan; Concert, a joint venture of British Telecom and AT&T that both preceded and survived those companies' merger talks; and a General Electric venture. We come back to some of these and other exchanges later in the book to lend practical insight to the proceedings.

Not all Internet solutions are particularly big, and the imperial solution is not always either comprehensive or sufficiently deep. So even if you're the chief executive officer of one of the top *anythings* in the world (and if you are, then your name has been in the press because you've "joined" or "committed" or "aligned"), then—even then—you can't rely on any one net market, because there are so many other markets that sound so good.

This book is written for you.

We can't claim to know the future, but we have worked closely with executives in industries facing these very to-join-or-not-to-join decisions, and we have also followed the rise, fall, and twirl-about of net markets since they first began to dance on the business stage. As a result, we have strong convictions about how companies that decide to join B2B online exchanges can position themselves—convictions that are sometimes counterintuitive. In this book we will discuss the following truths:

➤ *There is a learning curve.* One of the truths about net markets is that you need to use them in order to gain experience. That's the only way executives will be able to understand what you need to do to integrate your company's processes or take part in e-opportunities in a way that makes a material impact on your business. It's also clear that your net market investment may not earn your corporation money for a few years, particularly if you have legacy systems to overcome and training costs to be expended. But learning is transferable.

Part of our task is to shorten your learning curve as much as possible. This book includes discussions with executives throughout the world who are making net markets happen. It also includes the stories of net markets that have listened to their customers—that is, *you*—and quickly changed their value proposition in response to clearer thinking and a rapidly changing business environment. Their experience can help you leapfrog your competition.

➤ *The moment is now.* First movers may not always have the advantage (we'll return to that thought in Chapter 1), but it is clear that first provers will be in the best position to mold online exchanges to align with their own business strategies. Take Sara Lee Corporation. Not only did the company help design Transora, an Internet utility that serves the consumer goods industry, it also spun off former executive vice president and chief financial officer of Sara Lee, Judy Sprieser, to become CEO of the new net market. Any questions as to whether Transora knows how to make its important corporate founders happy? Anyone?

This book walks you through the steps needed to help you exploit existing and anticipated net markets and Internet utilities in your industry sector so that you can determine how well they align with your company's own strategies. It may be that, like Sara Lee, you'll decide to help start up an exchange (and even populate it with your own staff), but it also may be that you will find an existing net market that serves your strategic needs. But don't stop with just one e-market. Increasingly, companies are discovering that they are engaged with more than one market and more than one role: Founder, member, supplier, buyer—the corporate roles morph into one another with amoeba-like moves.

➤ *More than one successful net market model is emerging.* Net markets can have a few members, or they can be open to all comers; they can offer one service, or they can host many services. However, as our guided tour shows, certain characteristics are emerging as necessary for success. Most particularly, the industry-sponsored exchanges are gaining scope and scale, leaving their pure-play competitors in the dust ... and bankruptcy court. Consider EC Cubed, a B2B application services provider (ASP) that shut its doors after failing to secure $9 million in second-round financing. Its demise sent 250 staffers into the food-retail-services sector. We'll return to other differences between industry-sponsored and pure-play e-markets in Chapter 2.

➤ *All the rules have changed, and as you are reading this they are changing still.* You can't step into the same river twice unless you freeze it. And you can't freeze, or even chill, the Internet. Even net markets that are successfully up and running are already substantially changing their value proposition in order to keep up with the changing market.

PartMiner, for example, a provider of B2B procurement services to the global electronics industry and a specialist in sourcing and providing shortage components, struck an alliance with E2open, an electronics marketplace group whose members include IBM, Hitachi, Lucent, Nortel and Toshiba. The reason for the alliance: combined with PartMiner's sourcing for shortages, the member companies of E2open were able to address a major problem associated with supply-and-demand fluctuations that supply chains can't deal with on their own. The same week that deal was cut, Ventro, an early vertical marketplace operator, announced a shift in its focus from creating and operating wholly owned vertical marketplaces to becoming a service provider. David Perry, Ventro's president and CEO, calls the move a "natural evolution" that reflects a combination of transaction and service-based offerings. That's as natural as evolution from carbon-based life forms to copper-based life forms!

Cost advantages, one of the initial reasons for B2B markets, evaporate as inefficiencies are pushed out of the value chain, but this book shows how we know individual companies will balance participation in Internet utilities with unique customer services and branding opportunities to create real marketplace differentiation that will stand up over time.

What this book doesn't do is go too heavily into the technological components that make net markets work. The hardware and software is changing too fast for definition here, but we do talk about the fundamental issues, and fear not, we even explain the ins and outs of XML (extensible markup language) in plain English. (We perform that magic in Chapter 12.) We will also work to improve your awareness of the key questions and considerations you should ask when partnering with information technology providers. More critical to us are the strategic questions that will affect your organization's ability to make the right choices from among the many net market opportunities it will encounter—questions such as:

➤ What internal changes does your organization need to make to take maximum advantage of net markets? What about standards? Aren't they the enabler for a lot of this Internet stuff?

➤ How do net markets reshape your company's value chain? How can they redefine your industry sector?

➤ How can you maximize participation in net markets and make the right decisions while evolution is still in its infancy and its track record is nonexistent?

➤ How can you exploit your participation to reshape pricing issues and asset allocation?

> ➤ How will human capital needs change in the new economy? What role will knowledge management and innovation play?

> ➤ Looking beyond the early successes, what is the outlook for successful net markets two, three, or even five years into the future?

We share insider views with market makers that we believe to be most promising—those that have unique value propositions—and we provide insights from the executives who make them tick. We define several business models, from those with limited functionality and so are well suited to specialized products, to dynamic trading models that are better suited to global exchanges. We will also look at the advantages and disadvantages of vertical (industry-specific) versus horizontal (cross-industry) exchanges. Down the road, these markets may evolve independently, eventually developing interdependent links with other net markets.

Throughout the book, at the end of each chapter, we will provide a checklist of questions to think about and lessons learned that are designed to help you recognize genuine opportunities, assess the risk of entry, and perhaps suggest where best to establish your enduring partnerships.

Oh, and one more thing: As we finalize this manuscript and send it to the publisher, we know that it is light-years (in new-economy time) prior to when it will actually hit the shelves and you pick it up and read it. Given the ups and downs of the Nasdaq even as we write this paragraph, we promise to keep you updated with changes to the e-marketplaces highlighted in this book by putting regular updates on our web site < www.atkearney.com >. We look forward to seeing you there!

■ DOING IT THE OLD WAY

Of course, some things haven't changed at all in the new economy. It still takes the time-honored talents of good management to run a good company. After the deal is signed, after the technology enablers are in place, and after deployment and integration issues are resolved, sustainable value is a matter of leadership, commitment, customer relationships, something real to sell, and—as always—reliable execution. Without leadership, a commitment to innovation, and, above all, a sense of urgency, success will only be ephemeral.

Meanwhile, the noise outside your door is the trading opportunity of a lifetime moving swiftly forward. Your stakeholders are expecting no less than full involvement. So let's dive in.

Part

I

Expectations
and Realities

Market forces have changed the balance of power. Once upon a time (think Eisenhower), the supplier called the shots, but in the 1970s and 1980s the power moved to the retailer; in the 1990s, the balance of power moved to the consumer.

Remember when organizations suddenly discovered that the customer is king? Once the reality set in, world-class companies invested not-so-small fortunes in data capture and management to gain increasing information about their customers, and they marketed to progressively smaller customer groups—inevitably down to groups of one. Unfortunately, the vast number of these investments never resulted in the competitive advantage they targeted.

However, the goal of individual markets remains even while the bar is constantly being raised. Customers, both consumers and businesses situated along the value chain, increasingly demand more efficient, cost-effective—and individual—ways to do business. And companies continue to look to their information systems for answers.

Net markets are responding, even in the most traditional of industries. They are providing a value chain via e-links, and they are providing ways for suppliers and customers to come together directly through web-based trading platforms.

These platforms promise to level the playing field for all comers, both large and small.

To provide the efficiency that their customers demand is why new net markets cropped up so quickly in 1999 and 2000 and also why established firms signed on as partners. But getting traction in B2B commerce is not as simple as announcing a new market and putting out an "Open for E-Business" sign, as many e-markets learned to their chagrin. The latter may now seem obvious, but our research increasingly shows that throughout the heady days of Nasdaq heaven, incubator net markets spent more time planning their public relations (PR) campaigns and dreaming up killer Super Bowl ads than they did worrying about strategic goals, business strategies, or even staffing. The result: Those killer ads drained their bank account, and with no more venture capital to be had, these B2Bs went belly-up.

What's the future of business-to-business marketing? What's the right e-market for you? Which one will help you meet your organization's strategic goals? What questions should you ask in a sadder-but-wiser, but still inchoate, industry to ensure that you join a B2B that will develop a track record of market superiority and lasting value?

Log on to a net market's web site and in the "about us" section you'll inevitably find a self-published description that touts this particular market as best-in-class in its industry because it is horizontal or vertical, open or closed, even large or small. Maybe it offers a simple Internet utility or a full range of online services, but in either case, it claims that what is offered is definitely the best.

This leads to the $64,000 question: In a business world with no track record, with few identifiable brand names, and in which no one has yet made any money, what characteristics can you look for that will deliver on the promise of long-term profitability?

As in all things, luck goes to the vigilant.

In this case, vigilance requires understanding the different value propositions that these sites are using to go to market, as well as the requirements that our experience suggests are imperative for net market success.

In this section, we will examine the myths that have already grown up around net markets, and we will put to rest the hype and overblown expectations of what net markets can and cannot do. We'll look at the various models of net markets and discuss the inherent value propositions that each offers. Finally, we'll strip away the hype from that most popular of buzzwords—*ecosystem*—and although we'll show that the smartest distance between two points is no longer a straight line, we'll also show that ecosystems will take time to mature before they change the way business does its business.

Read on.

Chapter

1

Six Myths
of Net Markets

*When net mania hit full force early in 2000, it seemed that all
you had to do was announce a new e-market—and then wait
for the dough to roll in. Of course, it didn't work out that way,
but before the NASDAQ crashed and reality resumed, a lot of
misinformation on net markets and how they operate was cir-
culating freely. What's a net market, anyway? It's easier to
explain what it is not.*

Just as famed astronomer Carl Sagan was awestruck by the
"billions and billions of stars" in the universe, so today's
executives are reacting with equal awe to the trillions and
trillions of dollars that are expected to make up the world
of e-business. Nasdaq valuations notwithstanding, the Gartner Group predicts that by 2004, worldwide business-to-
business e-commerce will be in the stratosphere, topping
$7 trillion.

However, executives charting a course for the future
need to be less starstruck by the analysts' lofty predictions
and more focused on the real dangers as they navigate
through the world of B2B e-commerce. Companies are better served by a leader who can recognize and steer clear of
each blip that appears on the radar screen, rather than one
who contemplates the dazzling possibilities of the future

and who feels that trial and error will ultimately result in success.

In this chapter, we expose—and explore—six myths about net markets that have recently gained acceptance. It is our belief that, as net markets become more business-as-usual, the falseness of these myths will become more self-evident. At this time, however, the lure of new market opportunities makes these myths seem more real than reality itself.

■ MYTH 1: FIRST-MOVER ADVANTAGE IS CRITICAL

Who was the first person to reach the peak of Mount Everest? If you answered Edmund Hillary, it may be because even the history books give that quick but not-quite-complete answer to this question.

Twenty-nine years before Edmund Hillary made his historic climb to the summit of Mount Everest in 1953, George Mallory made his third and final attempt to reach the same peak. Tragically, on the day Mallory was to climb to the summit, he and his climbing partner disappeared on the mountain. Whether they made it to the top before they died remains a mystery. When reporters asked Hillary if Mallory's possible climb to the summit detracted from his own success, Hillary responded with a leadership truism: He said that to count, a successful climb to the top of Mount Everest also required a successful descent.

In other words, being first only matters if you survive to talk about it. First *prover* always beats first *mover*.

Comparing success in the business world to mountain climbing is nothing new: Making it to the top is the driving force for business leaders and adventurers alike, but as George Mallory's fate illustrates, focusing on the wrong goal can be fatal.

For companies worldwide, the goal has frequently been to gain first-mover advantage. Even the term *first-mover advantage* was coined by business historian Alfred Chandler to describe how corporate giants including DuPont, Procter & Gamble, Coca-Cola, and U.S. Steel harnessed technology and other inventions—notably the railroad—to build distribution and market share. Their initial investments—and existing infrastructure—were massive, giving them economies of scale and scope that ultimately helped them dominate their industries for decades.

First-mover advantage has been thought to be the goal for net markets as well. The market buzz and the attractiveness of being considered innovative outweighed whatever calls for prudence may have been heard. But staking out a URL (uniform resource locator) and distributing a press announcement are no substitute for the real thing. Although many first movers reaped the publicity of being first and maybe even plunked down megabucks for a Super Bowl ad, most weren't able to translate that publicity into customer loyalty or sustainable value. As a matter of fact, even after more than $3 billion in ad spend in the fourth quarter of fiscal year 1999, most net markets had negligible name recognition: Nobody knew what they really did. In their haste, they sometimes overlooked the fact that long-term prosperity requires more than just entering the market.

Amazon.com is the classic case. In the first years of the new economy, everyone wanted to follow Amazon's lead. It had successfully tapped into a new market before many people had even heard of the Internet or gone online. Although the backbone of the Internet had been in place since the 1960s, and the World Wide Web officially came online in 1991, surfing—at least the waterless kind—didn't become popular until the mid to late 1990s, and Amazon caught the first wave as it opened its doors in 1995.

Little did the offline competition realize that Amazon wasn't really selling books over the Internet, it was buying customers on the Internet with money it drained off of sector margin. By the time the established book chains finished increasing their discounts on everything, deciding what they should do on the Internet, and wondering what happened to the sector—the second huge revolution in 30 years—they could only dream about outdoing the upstart.

Clearly, the days of the Amazon-style rise to glory are gone: The heady days of skyrocketing stock prices and free-flowing venture capital have given way to eagle-eyed investors looking for solid long-term business plans. Even Amazon is learning that it needs to show more than purchases—it needs to show a profit.

The ongoing spate of dot-com crashes illustrates that the market has returned to the unforgiving fundamentals of business reality. In fact, the latest craze in web sites is encapsulated by those that have sprung up to document the failures. Sites such as the *Industry Standard*'s Dot-Com Flop and the now-defunct dotcomfailures.com (with its logo of "Kick 'em while they're down") made a sport of watching fallen entrepreneurs, many of whom had earlier laid claim to first-mover advantage. The George Mallorys of the online business world have suffered the same fate as the mountain climber: They made it to the top, but the downward trip was not good.

Within net markets, the story is much the same. Amex, for example, had first-mover advantage late in 1999 with its B2B Commerce Network service, which planned to help customers cut indirect expense and MRO costs. But the site failed to attract enough participants, and by August 2000, executives decided to bring in net market veteran Ventro (formerly Chemdex) to inject new life into company. The price wasn't cheap: Amex gave up operational control and a 35 percent stake in the company, now christened MarketMile, to Ventro. MarketMile is being reborn with a mandate to help midsize companies purchase industrial and office supplies, as well as professional services such as temporary labor.

The lesson learned for the fast-moving executives at Amex was that their company needed a partner with deep experience and knowledge of the net marketplace. We'll talk more about the requirements of B2B alliance building in Chapter 11.

This does not mean that time is not critical. Early movers can build brand and market share, all of which are important for success. But moving too quickly to market—without first building the right strategy—is a mistake that too many early B2Bs made. Our client work has taught us that basics count: A business plan, a pricing strategy, even hiring a qualified CEO is a rare event at more dot-com B2Bs than the press releases suggest.

What first movers can do is create a litmus test for a new market or sales channel, a test that can be examined by successor companies. Consider the story of online food exchange Efdex. Founded in 1994, Efdex sought to link food and drink distributors in the United Kingdom using Internet and satellite technology to provide real-time quotes, industry-focused television news, and market analysis on a secure trading platform. Target users were farmers, restaurant and bar managers, hotel-chain supervisors, and fish-market buyers. But by the fall of 2000, the company ran out of cash and had to close its doors. Efdex partner Lee Manning complained, "The concept never got the chance to prove itself. It was not up and running and the market for cash went cold." Efdex's bad luck with the market, however, will serve other companies that follow its lead into the food and drink distribution business.

The most important question that executives must think about is what they want to be first to achieve. First in the industry to go online? First to sell products online? First to achieve critical mass? Or first to achieve a sustainable profit? As with everything else, not all firsts are created equal.

■ MYTH 2: SIGNING THE DEAL IS A SIGNIFICANT MILESTONE

Judging by the number of deals that are announced in any given week, it would seem that the world of net markets is expanding exponentially. But signing the deal is the first—and often easiest—step in what frequently turns out to be a very short and fruitless journey.

A study conducted by e-business market analysis firm AMR Research in mid-2000 reported that of the online exchanges launched in the previous 18 months, more than 600 had yet to complete their first transaction. That's understandable; after all, it takes time to get up and running, even in the new economy. The study also revealed that none of the top exchanges came even "remotely close to approaching 1 percent of their respective industries' revenue." Again, a learning curve is to be expected, and a long-term approach is to be commended. Executives of the WorldWide Retail Exchange, for example, don't expect the exchange's activities to make a significant difference to the bottom line of member companies for at least one year after the exchange became functional in the summer of 2000. The AMR study also revealed that even those net markets that had achieved some level of liquidity had done so mostly via a small group of business customers. Chem-Connect, for example, received 44 percent of its 1999 revenues from only two sources.

The lesson is clear: It will take a while for the economics of the new economy to kick in.

"Few marketplaces are doing more than tens of millions of dollars in transactions a month," says Russ McMeekin, president of e-business for Honeywell, which is involved in MyPlant.com and MyAircraft.com and plans to launch MyFacility.com. "And most are close to zero in terms of procuring parts online," he said. At this point, he added, "everyone's exploring and testing."

Clearly there is a learning curve to participating in net markets. And taking full advantage of everything they can offer requires extensive changes within a company. It should be no surprise that many companies are starting their B2B operations with indirect purchases. They plan to procure paper clips and facsimile paper via the Net until they are comfortable with the learning curve. Only when they prove the procurement process with items that—let's face it—the company can survive without, will they branch out to electronic procurement of material necessary to keep the production lines running. By extension, this means that exchanges of direct goods may take a while to gain liquidity.

The promise remains worth the wait: Paper2print.com promises its paper industry clients a 20 percent to 35 percent reduction in order-processing costs and overall efficiency improvements of 3 percent to 12 percent, which it expects will be achieved through increased inventory turns, lower carrying costs on inventory, shorter cycle times, and improved use of working capital.

The efficiency improvement that a company actually achieves—will it be 3 percent? will it reach 12 percent?—largely depends on how the company aligns its own internal systems with that of the net market. We'll return to that theme in Chapter 10. But clearly, if a company simply uses paper2print's web interface, its efficiency improvements will remain on the low end, while competitors that adopt a completely integrated and collaborative planning and sourcing system will be in-line to achieve the higher-end numbers.

If we build it will they come? With all respect to Kevin Costner and his Field of Dreams, *it just ain't so.*

■ MYTH 3: IT'S ALL ABOUT TECHNOLOGY

Well, technology is clearly critical. Enchanting stories of net markets that boast an all-impressive, high-tech user interface sometime mask horror stories of back offices filled with people using hand calculators and fax machines because the software doesn't support the entire business process—merely the transaction. The fact is, some high-tech solutions may not be so high-tech after all. The online e-zine *E-Commerce Guide* reported in the summer of 2000 that most auction exchanges currently only take members through the price agreement; some even fail to offer background checks on the vendors.

Yes, if technology is a driving force of the new economy, you want to make sure that you are driving a Porsche, not a Yugo. But it's still *you* in the driver's seat, just the same. It takes a skilled, experienced driver to steer the car in the right direction; otherwise it will go nowhere, and certainly nowhere fast. In today's tight labor market, finding the best drivers is perhaps the greatest challenge companies face. CNET news reported that approximately 85 percent of net markets launched between the spring of 1999 and the spring of 2000 failed to become operational, largely because of chaotic staffing problems.

Shortage of human capital is an issue that also can be overcome by good business planning. The fact is, many analysts blame the shortage of talented people for the lack of substance—read, "poorly defined business plans"— behind many net market deals. After all, good talent will only go where they smell success.

Barbara Babcock, Unisys's president of e-business services, claims that many executives believe they can bring a net market online within 18 to 24 months. For most, however, this time line has proved impossible. Constantly changing business and technological models combined with massive employee defections have left many companies in critical condition before their first transaction even takes place. But given that business models and technology models will remain in flux, the best chance that executives have at achieving stability is to hold on to their employees.

In the ongoing battle for top talent, round one went to the start-up net markets. But as the Nasdaq fell, many dot-com millionaires discovered that their stocks were not destined to follow the path of Microsoft's. The *Wall Street Journal,* in fact, even ran a story on the ever-growing roster of the "90 Percent Club"—its name for those with the dubious distinction of having lost 90 percent of their paper worth. Now that the bloom is off the dot-com rose, old-economy firms are finding it slightly easier to attract and retain talent with their traditional, get-rich-slow career plans. Even so, retaining the best talent will not be easy.

If retaining talented employees is critical, that factor pales in comparison to the relationships that these employees craft with suppliers and vendors. In fact, the trust that your people build into their relationships, although critical in the old economy, becomes even more so in the new. Although today's economy boasts virtual marketplaces in which buyers and sellers can trade millions of dollars' worth of goods and services without exchanging a word, the death of personal business relationships has been greatly exaggerated.

Recent cases highlight the effect when long-standing competitors suddenly join net markets and become bedfellows. The online exchange Covisint, sponsored by GM, Ford, and DaimlerChrysler, is a case in point. All the XML-based technology in the world, for example, couldn't speed the process of choosing a name, which took the collection of CEOs and senior executives involved nearly three months to determine. Suffering from a severe case of too many cooks, making basic decisions became an ongoing game of tug-of-war. Nearly one year after the three partners signed on to create the exchange, they had yet to appoint a CEO and to agree on a permanent headquarters.

In every culture, personal relationships are the cornerstone of business transactions. In China, for example, companies are very slow to participate in net markets specifically because of the importance of personal contact in the business culture. Several companies, in fact, have begun to turn this dilemma to their advantage. MeetChina. com and Global Sources have each hired hundreds of people to travel the countryside to meet with business owners and encourage them to go online. Personal visits also allow for the chance of a close inspection of company processes and products. "When we looked at cross-border trade, there was a general lack of trust between buyers and sellers," says Len Cordinier, chief executive officer of MeetChina. "If you can use on-the-ground intermediaries to rate suppliers, it helps."

Another B2B company, Alibaba.com, hosts gatherings at trade shows at which online traders can meet offline and get to know one another. "The biggest problem is not technology or infrastructure. It's people's mentality toward doing transactions on the Internet," says Joe Tsai, Alibaba's chief operating officer. "Habitual behavior is hard to change, so we are focusing our efforts on making the online experience an extremely easy process for people to adopt."

■ MYTH 4: NET MARKETS ARE ALL ABOUT COST-CUTTING

The cost savings promised by net markets are, in fact, enticing. As net markets iron out the inefficiencies of the supply chain, all companies will be able to realize significant savings. However, when all companies enjoy the savings of B2B, the competitive advantage of the first movers will be eliminated. Transactional efficiencies, regardless of how large they are, are just the beginning of the possible advantages net markets have to offer. But their realistic implementation is still a fairly distant vision that is obscured behind all of the near-term cost-cutting opportunities and buried beneath the significant organizational changes required to use net markets at all.

Beyond cost reductions, net markets are also paving the way for dramatic, widespread changes that will be felt at all levels of business. As they mature, net markets will dramatically redefine industry structures to change the business models of the participants; they will also create new market opportunities by picking up the loose strands of previously bundled service offerings and putting them back together in interesting and valuable ways.

➤ Redefined Industry Structure

Companies can structure their net market relationships and alliances in ways that truly differentiate them in the market and, thus, can achieve a lasting competitive difference that will translate into superior returns. It's too soon to explore examples of companies that have successfully done this in the current wave of development, and for most companies, the needed strategies will be dramatically different than any they undertake today. But analogies from previous developments exist: When Henry Ford put the five-dollar day together with the Model T car, he created a new industry in the United States. Similarly, John Malek and Gerald Eskin put scanner data together with hard-edged analytics to reshape the market research industry with Information Resources, Inc. (IRI).

Not only will the organization change to take advantage of B2B opportunities, but business priorities will change as well. We will return to this theme later in Chapter 10; suffice it to say here that formulating the right strategic positioning and partnering strategies—before moving ahead—will be a prerequisite for companies to secure and retain long-term competitiveness.

➤ New Market Opportunities

Only a year ago, the business magazines were proclaiming that "e" would mean the death of the third-party intermediary. But intermediaries that add value will not only survive in the new economy, they will thrive. Three kinds of B2B market intermediaries have emerged that offer varying degrees of value:

1. *Relationship intermediaries* act primarily as online agents, connecting buyers and sellers in fragmented markets. Both buyers and sellers go to these web sites with the hope of either finding critical industry information or saving money. For example, an engineer

who needs information on fiber optics might visit verticalnet.com to read a long list of potential suppliers, obtain product information from buyers' guides and product directories, and peruse daily industry news articles.

Auction sites such as paperexchange.com and eBreviate are also relationship intermediaries, but they provide a singular service: People who participate in auctions do so to cut costs. This is where new suppliers, geographically remote suppliers, and economically hungry suppliers alike can meet the buyer online to negotiate prices and terms.

2. *Transactional intermediaries* focus on simplifying transactions between established buyers and sellers. Typically, these intermediaries position themselves between sellers of complementary products and a fragmented customer base. They ease communications by automating purchase orders, invoicing, and payment processes. For example, food operators who go to Instill's e-store can place a single order for a variety of products that are supplied by several different distributors. For a fee, typically paid by the distributors, Instill divides that single order and routes the pieces electronically to the most appropriate distributors—those that already deliver regularly to the food operator. Last year, Instill booked more than $1 billion in orders through the site.

Online intermediaries move along a developmental continuum. At a basic level, relationship intermediaries enter the supply chain for a brief time to introduce the players—or in the case of auction houses to draw out value—and then get out of the way. Transactional intermediaries do more—they introduce buyers and sellers and then use the power of the Internet to administer the sales transaction.

3. *Virtual distributors* blend aspects of both the relationship and transactional intermediaries by pulling

together a diverse group of companies, automating their transactions, and then managing the flow of goods and services. Thus, virtual distribution lies at the far end of the continuum of intermediary involvement.

Dell Computer has been a virtual distributor for years; it interacts with customers to tailor a system that meets their specific needs, and then it coordinates the acquisition and distribution of all the elements needed to pull that configuration together.

Also consider the example of orderzone.com, which was created by distribution powerhouse Grainger. Grainger pooled a variety of distributors—itself, Marshall, Cintas, Corporate Express, and others—onto a single site where customers go to order everything they need. Orderzone.com grew from Grainger's desire to make it easier for buyers who previously had jumped from one distributor's web site to another to find what they needed and to place their orders. In June 2000, Orderzone merged with Works.com, bringing together Orderzone's marketplace of MRO goods with Works's purchasing service.

All three types of intermediaries have an effect on the supply chain, although the extent of their impact varies. For example, relationship intermediaries work well where there is noticeable fragmentation between distributors and end buyers. In established businesses, their impact is less significant because the buyers and sellers are already known.

The effect of transactional intermediaries, on the other hand, can be more tangible. In the food industry, to return to an earlier example, food operators benefit from consolidating their purchasing, but the distributors often end up losing because they pay for the cost of the service. Consequently, distributors are scrambling to compete directly with the online intermediaries. Food service distributor Sysco is preparing to launch new software to compete directly with Instill's e-store, and other distributors in other industries are expected to do the same.

Transactional intermediaries that provide a needed service have the best chance for a long life, particularly those that target bulk producers in industries that churn out more product than is necessary. Steel producers, for example, are happy to sell to intermediaries like MetalSite.com because it gives them a way to quickly unload excess or inferior product that would otherwise end up in warehouses, reducing company profits. This is also the case in the power industry. Recently, a power company sold 40 reels of fiber-optic cable (that had sat in a warehouse for two years) for $1 million to a telecommunications company within two weeks of listing it on TradeOut.com.

■ MYTH 5: BUSINESS MODELS THAT ARE SUSTAINABLE TODAY WILL STAY THAT WAY

No, e-business is not a mature market. It is the growth opportunities that make B2B so exciting. But many of the experiences that even well-established Power Players will have over the next few years will be embarrassing, ugly, or downright foolish. It was the same with electricity, the telephone, and personal computers (PCs).

Most of the current B2B marketplace models, in which entire industries—including direct competitors—work together to iron out the kinks in the supply chain, offer tremendous savings over the shorter term. We have already shown in this chapter that the benefits of transaction efficiency will quickly become a community utility and cease to offer competitive advantage to any one player. Thus, it is clear that these models must evolve, or e-markets will *become* as exciting as the electric company.

And the new economy has given new meaning to the term *quick-change artist*. Unless a company can rewrite its business plan overnight, it won't last long. Consider Ventro.

As the darling of the net market industry, Ventro (then Chemdex) went public in July 1999, with revenues of less than $200 thousand and a market valuation of $1 billion. Three months later, its valuation tripled to more than $3 billion. Its stock price topped out at $234.00, only to crash to below $1 several months later. And Ventro was not alone in its fall from investors' grace; even B2B powerhouses Ariba and Commerce One experienced similar grief.

The reason? Companies were not joining—let alone using—net markets at even a fraction of the rate that analysts had previously predicted. Approximately 80 to 90 percent of all business goods and services are traded through long-term contracts that last one year or more. However, many net market business models are geared to take advantage of short-term spot markets. Thus, even if companies sign on to these net markets, they are limited to bringing 10 to 20 percent of their business on board in the near term. For net markets that rely on high transaction volumes, this has meant weak cash flows at best.

As a result, many net markets have begun to shift toward more sustainable business models. In fact, finding a better business model has become an ongoing—and, in some cases, an all-consuming—effort. Venture capitalist Matthew Cowan, an early backer of e-marketplaces including Ventro, defends the business-model makeovers. "People see it as a negative event when a model shifts—and in most cases improves—when in fact it is simply part of the cycle of building a large business," he said. "The companies [they] should be most concerned about are those that don't change."

Global Food Exchange is an online market for poultry, meat, seafood, produce and other food perishables that is fighting lower-than-expected transaction volumes by providing a broad range of services to its members. Its logistics system, for example, works to provide a seamless solution that gives users multiple logistic quotes, carrier selection, and booking and tracking information.

For many companies, however, restructuring will come in the form of merging or consolidating with another company.

In 2000 alone, there were 1,327 Internet-related mergers and acquisitions, totaling more than $116 billion. And as with most other trends in the new economy, this is just the tip of the e-berg.

■ MYTH 6: THE RESULTS WILL BE IMMEDIATE

Patience may be a virtue, but it's certainly not one many of us can lay claim to. As our fast-food lifestyle continues to thrive, so does our impatience: We get antsy waiting for microwave popcorn to finish popping; we tap our foot in annoyance as the automatic teller machine whirs before it spits out our cash; and we glare at our computer with disdain if it takes longer than 20 seconds to produce an image from a web site halfway around the world. In an era of immediate technological fixes, it is increasingly counterintuitive to think that some long-term solutions may actually require more time than it takes to knock out an e-mail.

While it is true that net markets promise speed and results, there is fine print beneath the headlines that can't be ignored. Truly, the benefits of net markets are conditional. Success depends on a variety of things. Some are within our control, and some are not. For example, does your company have the necessary technological infrastructure ready to communicate with the net market? Does the net market boast a membership of all your industry's heavyweights? And if all the heavyweights are members, are they able to come together in the same arena to work together effectively? Finally, are enough transactions being conducted through the exchange to achieve liquidity and the bargain prices it promises?

The answers to these questions will ultimately determine both the effectiveness of the exchange and the benefits that your company will derive from participating in it. Remember, these answers are also very much a work in progress; despite the ubiquitous tag line, "business at the speed of 'e,'" we are still at the beginning of a very long learning curve.

Consider also that many of the exchanges that are building their businesses today will not be around tomorrow. A recent study by Jupiter Media Metrix claims that of the 500 net markets in Europe in 2001, fewer than 100 will survive into 2004. The primary reason for this gross spate of failures? Most will simply fade away because they were unable to achieve a high enough volume of buyers and sellers. Don't blame the *participants* of these doomed exchanges, though. It is not their fault. Any net market that does not provide sufficient benefits to its participants simply will not have the volume to hold up its end of the bargain.

These are just some of the currently prevalent myths about net markets. There will be more. The fundamentals of success are already fairly well known, however, and we will discuss them in Chapter 2 and throughout this book. Ultimately, companies that derive the full range of benefits that net markets promise will be those that have chosen wisely, have invested the time and talent to make the net market work, and are willing to wait for results. When the haze clears, the net markets that are still thriving will be those that offer the best value proposition for all of their corporate members. The results will be timely, but they will not be immediate.

In Chapter 2, we will look at the most common types of net markets you will encounter—and which types are right for you.

■ QUESTIONS

What is your primary goal for joining a net market? Does your business model suffer in areas that can be improved through net market technologies: complexity, disaggregation, lack of collaboration?

Is your company prepared to take a long-term perspective regarding the impact of net markets given that the benefits will probably not be immediate? How prepared are your financial reporting systems to recognize benefits against expenses incurred by different departments, functional areas, or groups?

Is your staff flexible enough to deal with the changes necessary to fully implement a net market strategy? Is your organization deeply functional, or have you begun to cut across functions to provide process approaches to serving customers, planning capacity, and developing products?

Chapter

Power Players versus the Pure Plays

The independent (also known as pure-play or third-party) e-markets grabbed an early market lead—then took a beating from industry Power Players when they introduced their own net markets. What happened? For all the talk of the agility and neutrality of independents, there was one little flaw that often proved fatal: their inability to attain liquidity.

Liquidity is the magic that transpires when critical mass is set into motion. In case you think you've wandered into a physics text, think of critical mass as the ability to successfully lure thousands of customers into a new retail store on its opening day. Is the retailer wildly successful? It depends: Did those customers buy anything? And, more important, did they return to open their wallets on day two? Critical mass is the line around the block. Liquidity is the singing cash register.

Put another way, while *critical mass* relates to the number and size of participants in a net market, *liquidity* is the volume of transactions they conduct. The more business that actually gets funneled through the net market, the greater the benefits to participants. When has a net market achieved the magic boiling point of liquidity? The answer varies, depending on the size of the market; $100 million of transactions may be considered a highly liquid market for tires.com, but for autoparts.com it might spell financial disaster. For net markets that are big and broad, liquidity is unquestionably more difficult to achieve across all categories.

Neutrality, as the name implies, suggests a lack of bias in a market. The *pure-play* markets that began the B2B boom, led by the likes of Altra Energy and PaperExchange, are quintessentially neutral. Then the Power Players muscled in to make sure the markets were on their side. *Proprietary* net markets, such as Wal-Mart's RetailLink, are the ultimate in bias—but Wal-Mart brings a lot of instant liquidity to the game, so its e-market was a first mover as well as a first prover. While such an arrangement curries favor with the in crowd, outsiders (or those on the other side of the table) are generally lukewarm or skeptical about the deal. Most Power Play exchanges aim for the win-win in the hopes of attracting a larger audience.

In the end, while aspirations to both liquidity and neutrality are admirable, they are often conflicting as well. In essence, the quickest way to achieve liquidity is to recruit a huge block of buyers or sellers that represent a significant chunk of the industry. But guess what? These heavy hitters want to run the show, dealing a blow to the neutrality of the venture. The result can end up being a Pushmi-Pullyu, where members really don't collaborate on much other than reducing the cost of buying technology.

■ THE WILLIAM TELL OVERTURE

When pure-play net markets first arrived on the scene, they revolutionized the way companies do business with one another. These Switzerlands of the new economy appealed to a wide base of buyers and suppliers—a particularly useful strategy in fragmented industries that lack a concentrated base of power on either the buyer or supplier side. Pure plays also touted their nimble nature. Free of the apron strings of huge corporations, they planned to quickly develop and implement new strategies. They relied on their technological prowess and their capability to quickly reconfigure their sites, add service offerings, and retool their commerce functionality to respond to rapidly changing market conditions. Along the way, their founders and early investors planned to get rich.

That was prior to April 2000. When the Nasdaq went south, net markets including PaperExchange, ChemConnect, and BuildNet were forced to set aside their IPO plans. Wall Street's renewed obsession with profits and quarterly earnings didn't bode well for start-ups that couldn't promise to be in the black in the very near future. Around the same time, the 800-pound gorillas came onto the scene. The Power Players who had serious clout found that stealing market share from the independents was almost as easy as, well, stealing share from independents in all other sectors in which they had been successful.

Nearly every industry now has at least one coalition of sizable industry incumbents that banded together to form their own online marketplace. These coalitions often deploy very different strategies. Buy-side coalitions focus on making procurement faster and cheaper; sell-side marketplaces create a new Internet channel for their collective goods and services. After falling into a press-release black hole for some time, Power Play net markets are emerging, doing business, gaining strength, and producing revenue, and they are ready for a fight.

It appears they have already won. As the consortia gain strength, the news media recount closure after closure of pure-play net markets. FoodUSA.com, an online meat and poultry exchange, opened for business in April of 2000. It lasted less than a year. Upside.com reported in early 2001 that FoodUSA.com chairman Rod Heller attributed the failure to an industry-sponsored rival. Commerce Ventures, founded by such heavy hitters as IBP, Tyson Foods, Gold Kist, Cargill, and Farmland Industries, had no first-mover advantage—but it had the names and clout it needed. "Commerce Ventures froze the market," said Heller, who added that the coalition inspired a reaction among meat and poultry traders similar to that of "deer caught in the headlights." Potential participants weren't willing to make a move toward FoodUSA until they saw how Commerce Ventures would fare.

Some pure plays reinvented themselves—in many cases, more than once. Fob Inc., an industrial market maker that closed its high-profile Fobchemicals.com, Fobpaper.com, and Fobplastics.com, switched its focus in October 2000 to building a private marketplace platform, dubbed ProSource, that would let companies buy industrial materials direct online. But it has since bailed out of that business as well; it now focuses on helping companies comply with federal OSHA (Occupational Safety and Health Administration) standards. Federal regulations, it seems, offer a permanent port for a storm-tossed e-market.

Even Altra Energy, a clear leader among the independent energy exchanges, is under a double whammy of pressure these days. First, powerhouse Enron created its own Internet trading arm, making significant inroads into the market instantly. Then Enron's biggest competitors, including BP Amoco and Royal Dutch/Shell, joined to create Intercontinental Exchange. Analysts' predictions of a partnership between Altra Energy and a consortium abound.

The dominance of the industry-sponsored markets springs from several inherent characteristics. The most significant is critical buyer or supplier *mass*—which, as we mentioned, is a key ingredient in liquidity. The independents have to dedicate a huge chunk of time and money to persuade key industry incumbents to participate in their exchange. And there is natural resistance for a key player to support an upstart—why boost some pip-squeak's market cap with a press release? Consortia bring the party with them, however; they have commitments from heavy hitters and can often leverage their existing relationships and market muscle to solicit participation from other suppliers, distributors, and customers.

The most dramatic illustration is Covisint. Its players make up more than 70 percent of the automotive manufacturing industry; they barely break a sweat leveraging their industry power to solicit the support of key tier-one suppliers. In fact, Delphi and Meritor, two of the largest automotive suppliers, have agreed to participate, which puts Covisint—already strong on the buy side—in the fast lane to establish the sell-side liquidity it needs for a sustainable site (see Chapter 8).

And there's more. Many companies have been using electronic data interchange (EDI) for years. Although they have to translate this electronic communications mechanism to an Internet-based protocol, this task is much less daunting than creating a brand-new system altogether. The odds that big buyers and suppliers already have EDI in place are high, eliminating much of the need to sell the concept and create the process. Independents face a huge investment, not only to implement the new technology but also to create processes and persuade participants to use them.

Because the strengths of these industry-sponsored markets are tied in part to their not-insignificant influence, they shine brightest in consolidated industries where the coalition has significant control over some combination of product, distribution, customers, and suppliers. In industries where a few players hold most of these cards, one strong consortium can effectively bulldoze any pure play's hopes of striking up similar relationships. This is where the need for neutrality weakens somewhat. If enough of the industry participates in one coalition, fence-sitters may be swayed by the founders' collective control regardless of site bias.

Despite the efficiencies of a winner-take-all situation in which everyone flocks to that one magic market, the reality is that many industries are sharply bound by product, customer, and regional segmentation. The severity of these divisions, and the differences in industry structure and

power relationships within each segment, will determine
whether multiple online markets will be a necessity. In the
bigger industries, such as the $300 billion asset disposition
market, the playing field is spacious enough—for now at
least—for both types of players.

■ IT'S NOT EASY BEING SWITZERLAND

While consortia may be shellacking the pure-play models
in most industries, the game isn't over yet. The reason so
many pure plays are currently hanging on is that it takes
time to tackle the formidable obstacles associated with the
coalition model. Consider the following:

> ➤ *Neutrality considerations.* The fallout from fear of bias
> hits both buyers and sellers. Suppliers may hesitate
> to provide product and pricing information to a site
> controlled by Power Play suppliers out of reluctance
> to release critical information to competitors. Sup-
> pliers also understandably fear downward pressure
> on margins. If they are in the early stages of the sup-
> ply chain, they worry that they will be forced to take
> on more than they can reasonably accommodate,
> such as holding inventory that is currently held by
> buyers downstream. Buyers have issues to consider,
> too. Many are hesitant to disclose purchasing quan-
> tities and product specifications to a site controlled
> by other Power Player buyers, again concerned that
> sensitive information could fall into competitors'
> hands. Buyers want to be sure they won't unwittingly
> give competitors an edge while trying to sharpen
> their own. Parallel to the development of every Power
> Play net market is a redefinition of each Power
> Player's firewall.
>   Some net markets are responding to these con-
> cerns by setting up an independent third party to

manage confidential data. They are also developing technologies that give visibility to the entire supply chain. They are developing mechanisms for buyers to lock in prices and quantities. For example, EAN.UCC, the not-for-profit provider of UPC, EAN, GTIN, and SSC codes to 850,000 companies worldwide, launched UCCnet in June 2000 to address some of these concerns. The hallmark of this base release of UCCnet is to provide for synchronization of the data from the manufacturers, distributors, brokers, and retailers that will participate in the UCCnet community. This data synchronization is fundamental to all improvements and advanced collaborative applications that business-to-business e-commerce models aspire to implement.

UCCnet provides publishing authorization and subscription services so that suppliers can ensure that their data is synchronized with their authorized trading partners. Therefore, UCCnet users can be sure that the data they use to generate purchase orders (POs), acknowledge receipts, or share POS movement and forecasts is more accurate and timely. There's no fuzziness around which is right—UCCnet provides the second-by-second replay of who's on first. Therefore, you can't put last month's weight and cube on this month's PO because the synchronization process will prevent it. Sales reps and buyers will have to find something else to talk about for the first 13 minutes of their 15-minute meetings.

UCC has the advantage of being a not-for-profit outsider as well as the cachet of having successfully shepherded the UPC codes to their current universal prominence. UCCnet is furthering its leadership in establishing the global language of business through ongoing innovation and in its sponsorship of a host of initiatives, such as Global Commerce Initiative (GCI). GCI is assisting in aligning all the EAN.UCC parties' data-field standards and business-process requirements by sponsoring global pilots among select trading partners.

➤ *Antitrust concerns.* When industry titans get together, regulators take notice. For example, the Federal Trade Commission (FTC) scrutinized Covisint before giving the automakers' site the green light. The agency's goal was to determine whether the combined purchasing power of the automakers could be anticompetitive for suppliers. Antitrust considerations have not stopped, nor even substantially slowed, net markets as of this writing, but they call attention to certain principles any e-market needs to embrace. Avoiding competitive harm is the key to getting a passing grade from the FTC or the European Commission. In other words, net markets cannot be used to fix prices or output, to rig bids, or to share or divide markets by allocating customers, suppliers, territories, or lines of commerce. Antitrust is also judged by "rule of reason," which focuses on how an e-market might harm the state of competition versus the environment without that marketplace. Independent governance and procedures for safeguarding sensitive information are musts. An interesting twist in the antitrust tale: When the Power Players first started their initiatives in early 2000, the focus was on one big competitor talking to another big competitor; by the end of 2000, however, the concern shifted to two Power Play exchanges talking to each other and dividing up the Internet market sector. Regulatory vigilance can be nimble, too!

➤ *Coordination issues.* It's hard enough to agree upon a press release, and that much more difficult to reach a meeting of the minds on the strategic direction of a joint marketing venture. Think of all the details to be ironed out, including ownership structure, management structure (including the chief executive), site strategy name, content, design, and technology partners. Now multiply these delicate issues by the intense rivalry in many industries, in which potential collaborators are historically archenemies. Can you imagine Procter & Gamble (P&G) and Unilever working side by side to create a net market? And yet they are both on the board of Transora, the fast-moving consumer goods manufacturer exchange. The complications of coordinating such a net market range from a slowdown (where speed is a key objective) to an unraveling of the entire venture.

■ ALPINE RANGES

So industry-sponsored exchanges have the muscle in industry-specific e-markets. But not all online markets cater specifically to one type of business. This brings us to another basic way to categorize net markets: by the nature of what they sell. Need new computers for the office? Or are you in the market for cotton for your new line of shirts? Different exchanges are set up for each need; each has its own benefits and challenges.

Cross-industry markets, or *horizontals,* can help buyers reduce the purchase price of goods and services including MRO. In theory, companies can access a larger, more competitive supplier base, leverage buying power via consortia, and capitalize on spot-buy opportunities due to market imbalances. Online auctions create even more competition and drive-down prices—although sellers will have to recoup their losses somehow. Profit-hungry participants can super-size their buying power if they band together, and buying consortia can wield 5 to 10 times the buying power of an individual company. Horizontal net markets can be an effective way to rein in maverick buyers within your organization, too, by making preapproved items available to employees in an online catalog.

While the *vertical* markets (the ones that operate within a particular industry's value chain) also offer better prices and lower transactional costs, their ultimate goal is to improve supply-chain performance. When you can synchronize production and selling plans, you can cut inventories, as well as production, handling, and transportation costs. Creating a shared production pipeline between the company and its key suppliers will also increase customer service and satisfaction. Collaborative design systems can chop costs, speed products to market, and expand a company's knowledge of, and access to, potential design partners. Remember, in the future, the value chains will own the companies—not the other way around.

Vertical markets are positioned to make a greater impact on the way we do business. One reason is that they deal with direct materials, or goods used in manufacturing a product, typically representing up to 80 percent of corporate purchases. In addition, the value-chain efficiencies that collaboration will eventually yield are where the biggest gains will eventually be uncovered. The downside is that vertical markets pose a far bigger headache in terms of buying and execution.

Why? At the heart of the problem is the complexity of buying and selling direct materials. These goods are the life's blood of a manufacturing operation. Slight price increases in just one component can trash a company's bottom line. If the quality of a part is different than what is specified—for better or worse—the end product suffers, too, or the production line suffers from the hiccups. And consider the level of information, coordination, and collaboration that go into this process. Buying decisions are made item by item, based on the availability, discounts, terms, or specifications of other items. Given the intricacies of the business, deep industry knowledge is absolutely critical. Only those net markets that intimately understand the inner workings of your production processes can effectively bring the purchasing process online and streamline the supply chain. So what should you look for to ensure these complexities are being effectively managed?

➤ *Prescreening and certification.* Most likely, you're not thrilled at the idea of buying from an unknown supplier, especially when the continuous operation of your assembly line depends on getting exactly the right product precisely on time. Net markets that offer features such as quality standards profiling (think ISO 9000), manufacturing method identification and design capability categorization can dramatically increase your comfort level and decrease your blood pressure when it comes to new supplier relationships.

➤ *Automating negotiations.* With software from companies like Menerva Technologies, Commerce One, Oracle, and Ariba, net markets will be able to conduct multiparameter negotiations online, comparing offers and counteroffers and even exporting the agreed-to terms into an online purchase order or other purchasing document.

➤ *Online capabilities start to finish.* Many transactions initiated through a net market must be completed offline. That means that paper-based inefficiencies might be reduced, but they're not going away. Take the issue of payments, for instance. Companies including Clareon, Aceva, TradePayment, and Visa are beginning to automate the negotiation of payment-terms, payment-contract administration, and cash-management processes and to provide access to transaction-relevant financial services, such as accounts receivable financing, foreign exchange, currency hedging, and trade finance and insurance products. The most convenient e-markets will offer a range of additional support to fully automate the purchasing process, including logistics, order tracking, and legal services.

➤ *Visibility.* The ultimate goal of vertical net markets is to give participants enough supply visibility that they can quickly determine manufacturing capacity and inventory. Companies including i2 and lesser-known Redknife believe buyers' enterprise resource planning (ERP) systems will someday talk to suppliers' ERP systems through net markets, and these companies are developing applications to provide this function. With T2T (thing-to-thing) communication, orders would be automatically issued when inventories of a particular item run low. These orders will be sent to qualified suppliers on a continuous basis—or, more properly speaking, future shipping schedules would be continuously modified up to the manufacturer's specified lock-down date. Companies such as webMethods provide the connectivity platform for applications to talk with each other across the firewall, while other companies such as Arzoon and Supply Solutions execute supply-chain activities based on event management and business logic. Although online offerings that are not integrated to this level may provide a short-term method of sourcing direct materials, manufacturing companies will no doubt look for integration when they select their long-term sourcing partners.

In the end, no matter what the net market needs to do well—manage complexity, offer one-stop shopping, or bring new meaning to the word *visibility*—it must have an absolutely clear understanding of what your company buys and how you buy it. The net market that knows what you *really* need to gain competitive advantage and gives it to you on time, every time, makes the perfect partner.

Careful readers will have noted that this chapter pushes the meaning of the word *industry* to its limits. In the e-enabled economy, the value chain that produces a manufactured product includes everything from the raw materials to manufacturing and distribution services to postsales support. Are all these players part of your industry? And let's not stop with direct links. Are you part of the paper industry just because your offices seemingly use reams of the stuff? The development of net markets rewrites the rules of just what makes up an industry and who your competitors are—and thus, ecosystems of industries are evolving. We'll explore this theme in Chapter 3.

■ QUESTIONS

Given that a comfort level with technology is necessary for entry into net markets, how high is the computer use among your industry's front-line buyers and sellers? Are their relationships defined by fact-based analysis and communication? What will need to change?

Are you concerned about disclosure of sensitive information to the net market you may join? Are independent parties available to manage this type of information and facilitate a net market for you? What *really* provides competitive advantage?

What antitrust issues could arise from a net market in your industry? Do you understand the risks and implications?

What must the net market offer to do (for example, manage complexity, provide one-stop shopping, increase visibility) to be of most value to you and your industry sector?

Chapter

3

Ecosystems

The Smartest Distance between Two Points

Metaphors help us see patterns in the universe. Sports and war metaphors have traditionally been used to describe a business world of brute force—of scale, mass markets, financial clout. That world is quickly receding, and other metaphors from physics and the natural sciences are more useful to describe how new-economy value is created and sustained.

The past few years have seen a big increase in the use of new terminology that has emerged around the business-to-business e-commerce reality. In every field or discipline preceding net markets, the rationale has been the same: The terminology is, in essence, practical shorthand of standardized language to mean the same thing to everyone communicating to each other about the subject. Okay, consultants who want to exclude outsiders from the conversation may overuse it, but ideally it helps put an end to linguistic confusion.

Business terminology brings order or context to communication, and requires fewer words. For instance, just picture trying to describe the semicircular area over an archway that's flanked and supported on either side by vertical members (columns) and a horizontal member (lintel) between the two. It so happens that there is a single word to describe this area. It's called a *spandrel*. It means one of two things in architecture according to the Random House Webster's *New World Dictionary:* (1) an area between the extradoses (exterior curve of an arch) of two adjoining arches or between the extrados of an arch and a perpendicular through the extrados at the springing line (a horizontal line between the springings of an arch), or (2) in steel-framed buildings, it refers to the panel-like area between the head of a window on one level and the sill of a window immediately above it. Our point: Probably no one but an architect or builder needs to use *spandrel* early and often in everyday speech, but for them, the word is basic to common understanding.

Business-to-business e-commerce is no different, and it needs new shorthand to describe the concept or feel of new business and commercial situations that are becoming increasingly complex. Sometimes terminology is created to describe anticipated complexity that hasn't quite been played out yet. Finally, the terms—sometimes called *jargon* and frequently involving acronyms—are borrowed from other disciplines in the hope that their application to new business models might give us more insight into what is, or should be, going on.

Thus, the cyberpunks have taken over and given new meaning to already useful nouns including *stream, surf, worm,* and *spam.* If you just love this stuff, check out the Glossary at the end of this book.

It should be no surprise that the biological sciences term *ecosystems* is being used to describe how communities behave and that application of the concept and terminology of quantum mechanics helps describe how Power Players are beginning to communicate. This chapter examines these two concepts—not to claim that they are right nor to revel in the jargon, but to examine if these ideas can shine more light on where the B2B revolution is going and how it will affect your company's business.

■ OUT OF THE RAINFOREST AND ONTO WALL STREET

Webster's tells us that an ecosystem is "the complex of a community of organisms and its environment functioning as an ecological unit." In this model, organisms imply growing, changing entities (companies) that consume and generate energy (money) in an environment (value chain) that impacts, and is impacted by, the organisms (other companies) that exist in it. James F. Moore defined the term *business ecosystem* in the mid 1990s as "an economic community supported by a foundation of interacting organizations and individuals—the organisms of the business world." He also emphasized that "the classical view of competition has become too simplistic. Instead of merely competing head-to-head within their industry, corporations are becoming linked into ecosystems that often span multiple industries." Clearly, there's nothing new under the sun.

A few years later, IT/management guru James Martin proposed that "when executives think in terms of ecosystems rather than one industry, they can play a grander game, often with higher return on investment," and that "as business ecosystems evolve, a major key to business success will be the invention, development and nurturing of business relationships." At least at a high level, this concept makes sense—it is consistent with the comment that in the future, value chains will own their companies and not the other way around. That's because the places along the chain where value is created are defined by consumers (or whoever is providing the value to the chain) and not by the producers (who, interestingly, are increasingly seen not as creating value, but as absorbing it in the form of costs and profits). Thus, consumers define the places where companies want to be, and increasingly define the value chains that serve them with less and less waste—regardless of what producers think. The Internet accelerates this trend, so let's walk around the new ecosystem and see how it fits our anticipated new world.

Just like an ecosystem in nature, activity in the Internet economy is self-organizing. The process of natural selection takes place around profit to companies and value from customers. Companies come together to offer a common technology, service offering, or customer focus to capture consumer value. As the Internet ecosystems evolve both technologically and in numbers, it will be even easier and likelier for companies to participate in the new economy. Unlike the traditional value chain, which rewarded exclusivity, the Internet economy is *inclusive* and has low barriers to entry. Already, $1 trillion in technical infrastructure is in place, ready and available for anyone to use at any time—free of charge. That's why new ideas and ways of doing business can come from anywhere at any time in the Internet economy. But a word of caution: It's as easy to exit as it is to enter. The companies that thrive will be those that find the points of value on the Net and exploit them.

Still stuck in the language? Perhaps an example will help. Today, a number of firms typically perform only one or a few activities along a given value chain. Thus, in the mobile phone business, Qualcomm is one of the companies that owns the enabling technology, Hewlett-Packard helps provide services, and Nortel is one of the firms that provides the infrastructure. A fully evolved mobile phone ecosystem, however, would include companies that provide mobile services (such as Verizon), companies that provide mobile access (AT&T and MCI WorldCom), companies that provide mobile appliances (such as Palm), and the list goes on and on. Interestingly, most B2B marketplaces today are set up around current value-chain interfaces—not future ones. Those Power Players that devise new interfaces that essentially rethink the value chain and create webs of new value will be the winners in an ecocentric world.

The parameters that make up an Internet-based ecosystem are becoming increasingly clear. They include:

➤ *Internet-enabled services.* If the Internet is the environment, then this is a baseline attribute. Web-based systems increase market reach, lower barriers to entry, and support (at least the concept of) real-time transaction processing. As the ecosystem develops, the Internet represents the environmental constraints or opportunities that act as a catalyst for mutation and evolution of the organisms.

➤ *Self-organizing capabilities.* Once established, the ecosystem begins to act spontaneously. It's no longer a linear connection. The value chain becomes disaggregated and then reconstructs itself in new ways either by creating new interfaces or new players or by rebundling parts of traditional players. Members come together as self-organizing teams to create new value or new efficiencies in the value proposition. In other words, the optimum distance between points is no longer a straight line.

➤ *Fluid and changeable.* Relationships are much more fluid in an ecosystem than in a traditional industry partnership, primarily because they are less likely to be defined by sharing of capital—working, human, or otherwise. They are also less well defined in terms of how they work together, and they are subject to frequent change without the trauma or costs of disengagement we have come to expect. Alliances form quickly and they can unform just as quickly; collaboration is useful, and competitive advantage is determined more by time than by position.

➤ *Adaptable.* As transaction platforms migrate to added-services platforms, the technology needs to adapt as well. We're talking about more than fluidity inside the net market with communication between members and along the supply chain—the intermarket dynamics—we are talking about fluidity in the intramarket, from exchange to exchange (E2E). For instance, MyAircraft.com has a platform that sits on top of the ERP systems of its member companies. Whether the ERP system is from Oracle or SAP, the platform for replacement parts must work seamlessly with the data forms and formats of those internal systems, making it easy for new members that have those ERP legacy systems to ramp up and do business with MyAircraft.com. You could think of this as a symbiotic relationship with a parasite or as similar to how some bacteria produce valuable chemicals in the organisms they invade. However, bacteria sometimes kill their host organism—which is why we still recommend use and stress tests for new systems!

➤ *Integrated.* Micro-vertical and horizontal net markets partner with one another to create higher value offerings. The idea is to find the points of value in the ecosystem and mine those points for everything they are worth. For example, E2open has allied with PartMiner in an E2E partnership between an industry-sponsored vertical e-marketplace and an independent B2B trading exchange. E2open is a collaborative e-marketplace whose founding members include a pantheon of global gods in the electronics industry. By combining PartMiner's transaction technology, a catalog of over 12 million electronic parts, and market-making offerings with offerings from its other technology partners, Ariba, i2, and IBM, E2open gives its customers a complete supply-chain solution. E2open is quickly realizing its vision of linking collaborative design tools with supply chain and open-market services. A recent A.T. Kearney study of electronic exchanges leads us to project increasing levels of collaboration in this space as exchanges look beyond transaction fees to collaboration and other services as a means of providing value differentiation. When this happens, the technology components and choices will need to be interoperable or combined into one. By playing an increasingly valuable role in the ecosystem, a participant makes itself more dominant and less likely to be destroyed by commoditization (the struggle for survival).

➤ *Made up of smaller ecosystems.* Just as organisms are born, grow, and die, so do ecosystems. Big ecosystems can be thought of as being made up of an interlocking chain of smaller ecosystems. In nature, use and conservation of energy determine what lives and what dies. In business ecosystems, a company's ability to add value to (or, more properly, extract value from) the value chain determines whether it will continue to flourish, or whether the value chain will select (as in, natural selection) another company. The depth of service provided by networked electronic marketplaces determines who the survivors will be.

Again, an example is timely: IT and communications companies have been putting together packages of tools in ASP format to give their customers the ability to dynamically manage the processes that they previously called in the IT experts to do for them. MCI, in concert with Cisco Systems, is offering a bundle that gives customers the power to manage bandwidth in asynchronous transfer mode (ATM)—essentially, to put up and take down lines when they need them. The package allows customers to self-manage communications, call centers, storage and network capabilities and, in effect, to create their own integrated information ecosystem. Because it contains a great deal of data about these customers, it provides this information to communications and networking companies. And because the communications and networking equipment companies are the experts in communications management, with this information they can help those customers do a better job of managing their communications needs, and in the process, of course, they deepen their relationships or connection with the customer. It's a virtuous cycle win-win-win, and in effect, these companies become ecosystems themselves all within a larger ecosystem.

➤ *Market intelligence and information.* The perfection of information flows in the ecosystem will lead to better product and service fits as the system searches for enhanced value. Let's say you're a user of airplane undercarriage axle grease. Ultimately, the intelligence that develops around the market through buying and selling in your B2B exchange will allow you to determine what you've been paying for the past six months, how that compares to expected and future market pricing, and what the spot market is for the stuff. Remember, all this information sits on your exchange server—in actual bits and bytes, or virtually through connections to other servers. You post an RFQ and in comes a new seller from Hungary quoting you a price that's half of what you've historically paid. Ordinarily, you wouldn't consider doing business with an unknown vendor, but thanks to the B2B exchange and its standards, integrity, and other asset-protection features, including currency translations, payment and vendor history files, you feel more comfortable in completing the transaction, realizing the significant savings and leveraging the exchange for greater reach. All this is happening now. However, without the more sophisticated capture and categorization of information, the broad application of the next level of evolution is unachievable.

In late 2000, Living Systems AG announced a collaborative effort that would create an ecosystem in the European steel industry. The German software developer's new partners include Metal TradeNet, virtual clearinghouse CapCLEAR, and logistics marketplace TradeNetOne. The deal is designed to provide customers with comprehensive service offerings ranging from contract negotiation, financing, and delivery. The idea is that buyers and sellers negotiate transactions on MetalTradeNet's platform, and receive free real-time bids for transportation through TradeNetOne. CapCLEAR processes the transactions, generates binding contracts, and takes care of risk management and credit. CapCLEAR also monitors the physical delivery, facilitates payments, and offers vendor ratings.

So far, so good. But the alliance isn't satisfied; it is already moving to embellish the system. "We are working very intensively to incorporate our customers' ERP systems into MetalTradeNet so that we can provide a complete picture of the value chain. Integration throughout the entire procurement process will provide users with enormous potential benefits in cost-effectiveness," says cofounder Andre Radebach. Sustainability will call for integrated links to the customer as well as at the company-facing end of the value chain.

What's next? A logical development in business ecosystems can occur wherever operating platforms promise greater results when joined together rather than when kept apart. The ability and ease with which this joining can take place with Internet-based solutions is what make the ecosystem metaphor so apt. For example, Commerce One, Ariba, and i2 Technologies could conceivably connect all the exchanges that use their technology platform, thus broadening potential offerings and services while hurdling the technology infrastructure cost and interoperability challenge in a single leap. If they were to do so, competitors would become collaborators—but in an ecosystem, organisms (companies) can have multiple roles without losing their focus.

■ SWINGING FROM VINE TO VINE

While the ecosystem metaphor is useful to clarify how business may need to operate in the Internet-fueled value chain

of the future, it also helps make clear what an ecosystem—
and this new business environment—is *not:*

> ➤ *Putting your business on the web.* Just like an alien
> creature plopped down in the middle of a swamp,
> cutting a deal that shoves your business onto an
> Internet platform will not make it a part of an
> ecosystem. An ecosystem has an impact on how
> business will be done as much as an environment
> has an impact on the health and strength of its resi-
> dent organisms. A business won't fit into the ecosys-
> tem until it reinvents the way it does its business,
> relates to its customers and suppliers, and commu-
> nicates information—in other words, how it lives in
> the Internet environment. We'll return to this theme
> in Chapter 10.

> ➤ *Transaction-efficiency efforts aimed at taking cost out of
> the business.* Hibernation may be a good way to get
> through the winter, but it's no way to live. Taking costs
> out may be a good way to make the quarterly earnings
> report, but it's no way to grow. It is true that the Inter-
> net provides opportunities to reduce costs and speed
> up transactions, but the Internet-based ecosystem
> offers a lot more, and higher-order organisms will take
> advantage of those opportunities. It's a given that play-
> ers will make the transactions that offer the greatest
> available efficiency, but that won't provide them with
> much added value in the long run. Remember that
> transaction costs—and transaction revenue—approach
> zero in the Internet-based ecosystem model. However,
> some companies, including Metreo, provide short-
> term cost savings in transactions while focusing on
> delivering new top-line revenue.

The discussion of what an ecosystem is and how it will
affect our business realities will probably continue for
some time, but meanwhile, front-running business leaders
are already employing this model in their business devel-

opment plans. "We're already much of the way there," Cisco Systems CEO John Chambers told *Fortune* magazine earlier this year. About 70 percent of Cisco's hardware goes directly from the company's interconnected partners who make the products to customers, without a Cisco employee ever handling any goods.

■ UMBRELLAS IN THE MONSOON

True business ecosystems—such as the Living Systems AG model described previously—are still regaining their equilibrium after the meteor that struck the Nasdaq catapulted them out of their petrie dish and into the unforgiving world of the Power Players. But the Power Players need to redefine themselves, too. For a true ecosystem to develop, it must have more than just a network of partners. It needs those partners to refigure out what role they will play, how they will manage internal systems and external alliances and relationships, and how they will coevolve in the B2B environment they've imagined into reality. Otherwise, the ecosystem won't find its equilibrium, and its organisms will not survive. Business ecosystems exist today, of course, but they are based on models that are rapidly changing. Transitioning to a new ecosystem is always a challenge.

Technology companies come closest to visualizing the totally interconnected experience they can assemble for their customers. In the spring of 2000, IBM, Ariba, and i2 Technologies announced a partnership to help users put together an integrated e-marketplace, with an e-procurement supply-chain system that allows them to carry out all the processes from placing orders to fulfilling them, as well as more tightly integrated processes involving users, suppliers, and the market.

"Today, businesses work with other businesses very inefficiently," says i2 Technologies CEO Sanjiv Sidhu. "For instance, over the last four years, companies have reduced their inventories by 50 percent. But where did that inventory go? To their suppliers. Their entire ecosystems haven't really benefited," he says. "We can change that."

And change is already underway. First, IBM integrated i2's TradeMatrix marketplace and Ariba's business-to-business e-commerce platform with its existing technology and deployed it across Big Blue's operations worldwide to manage the blue chip's whopping $45 billion annual procurement spend. In addition to achieving sizable savings and improvements in IBM's own procurement operations, the partners plan to develop and market a full range of e-market solutions to their clients.

As big as that is, that's just IBM's and i2's clients. The boundaries of the business ecosystem envisioned by James Moore extend beyond market intermediaries and their customers to include consumers, market intermediaries in its broadest sense—including agents and channels as well as those who sell complementary products and services—suppliers, and, of course, back to the company itself. It also includes the owners and other stakeholders of the organizations involved, the so-called primary species of the ecosystem, plus species that may be relevant in a given situation. Included in this zoological collection are government agencies and regulators, associations, and standards bodies representing customers and suppliers. Then there are the direct competitors and companies that compete with the initial company and with the other members of the community. In other words, Moore envisioned a rich mix of animalia that can be seen as the "flora and fauna that make up a particular ecosystem."

■ THE FAST WILL EAT THE SLOW

The business ecosystem is galactic and microcosmic at the same time. Ramsey Theory states that complete disorder is impossible—what seems like disorder is just a lack of sufficient scale. This is particularly true in the if-only-I-had-known world of business. Whether we know it or not, each of us has purchase intentions that are relevant to the companies that serve us. But without a mechanism for reporting this information—so that it can be captured and accessed throughout the enterprise—a link is missing between the company and the customer. How preposterous this sounds in the world of the ecosystem!

This is the vision that Internet-enabled ecosystems hold for us. For example, i2 Technologies has announced a joint venture with an e-marketplace in Malaysia called Planet-OneInc. Its mission is to electronically link—via i2 software—the remote forests in Malaysia with lumberyards in the United States. According to i2, this will cut the costs of home building in half. In the words of i2 CEO Sidhu, this represents "the next Industrial Revolution, benefiting the entire world's business ecosystem."

Is Sidhu overindulging in rhetoric? Or is this electronic link the proverbial canary in the mineshaft for a lot of built-in middleman costs that we, as homeowners, currently take for granted? It's too soon to know. Much still needs to evolve in the business ecosystem, but certain aspects of ecosystems are becoming clear:

➤ *The path to the customer is no longer a straight line.* In the e-commerce ecosystem, value creation is networked rather than hierarchical. Organisms within the ecosystem coexist and coevolve interdependently.

➤ *The laws of thermodynamics apply.* Energy must be conserved within the system. In the business ecosystem, that energy is money. The only source of money in the value chain is from the consumer; everybody else only borrows it for a little while.

➤ *Natural selection drives evolution in the ecosystem.* As in nature, business organisms evolve in response to their environment. At some points, evolution can be discontinuous, and Power Players become food for worms. The more profound the external influence on an ecosystem (meteor, comet, Internet technology), the less likely that dominant organisms will survive the cataclysm. IBM partnered with Ariba and i2 Technologies to power up the new electronic marketplaces and leverage their alliance into a sustainable advantage in streamlining various sectors of the economy. Two years from now the partnership may expand to include others—or the triumvirate may disengage and reengage with other players to gain or maintain new advantages in the evolving business ecosystem.

"A biological metaphor will help businesspeople to start acting from a much deeper understanding of their own New World," claimed Arie P. DeGeus, the Royal Dutch/Shell scenario-planning guru and author of *The Living Company*. Moore published his theories on ecosystems five years ago, but with a menagerie this size, it is clear that we have yet to experience the profound effect these theories will have in the Darwinian world of e-commerce. Still, we may not have to wait another five years; B2B commerce may still be relatively young, but it is progressing to maturity at light speed. And as one tech executive puts it, on the Internet, "the fast will eat the slow."

As we go to press, there are well over 1,000—some estimates run closer to 2,000—active or soon-to-be net markets or exchanges on the web. That's just a start. AMR Research predicts the number will multiply to 5,000 over the next several years. AMR Research also predicts that 95 percent of the total will vanish through mergers, consolidation or, more likely, bankruptcy. Along the path to solvency or bankruptcy, several sustainable business models will evolve. At the end, we will look back and realize that the path that started with clay tablets moved through the telephone and fax to EDI, transitioned to seller and buyer solutions and then to B2B net markets and e-hubs, until finally, true e-commerce ecosystems emerged.

What will those business models look like? We don't have complete knowledge, but we do know what the characteristics will include. We'll study those characteristics in detail in the next section of this book.

■ QUESTIONS

What value-chain ecosystem(s) is your organization currently a part of? Where does the real money come from? Who spends that money? Do you really understand where all 100 pennies your consumer spends on your product go? Be careful—there is nothing in your own accounts that gives you this answer.

Is there value in migrating into other ecosystems? Asked another way, is there another stream of money that you can stand in and get some? If so, what is it? If you're a Power Player, chances are you have a lot of options—you can do a lot of things that other (less evolved) organisms would be anxious to pay you for. How can you get involved without losing focus?

Given that the evolution of an ecosystem is organic, dynamic, and unpredictable in nature, what steps can you take to mitigate the risk associated with this uncertainty? How is your organization arranged to deal with this kind of risk—is it organized by potential result or likely cost? What are the interface points in the ecosystems in which you participate around which a new connection method could be developed that would provide a significant value proposition? What's your Napster?

Part II

Building the B2B Foundation

One of the lessons of the 1990s was that scale would create a category killer that could rock the rules of competition in a given industry. We all watched as Borders rewrote the book industry, IKEA redesigned the furniture-market supply chain from end to end, and Wal-Mart effectively took a wrecker's ball to Main Street, USA, retailers. But if e-markets have the effect that their adherents claim, in a few years we will all be competing in a drastically different environment, in which scale can be created via partnership—a lot faster and a lot cheaper than your typical merger or acquisition.

Consider that as the millennium dawned, Wal-Mart was the largest retailer on the planet; within a few months, it ranked number three, because the WorldWide Retail Exchange and GNX, net markets backed by serious Wal-Mart competitors, both opened their doors in 2000. There is a saying that if Alaska were cut in half and two states were created, Texas would suddenly rank third; with the advent of net markets, the retail strategy framework of format/business system/scale turned into just format/business system.

It's not just Power Players that will benefit from this realignment of scale in the e-market environment. Kingfisher's David Jobson, one of the founding members in the WorldWide Retail Exchange, puts it pointedly: "If the

WWRE is a truly open exchange, smaller competitors will take part in it. We are in effect promoting them." As to handling the natural objections to helping smaller competitors grow into large ones, he explains, "We need to say that this is open to everyone, but your ability to exploit it will depend upon your creativity and involvement."

So scale and critical mass are, well, critical. In fact, in an A.T. Kearney study last year of executives representing more than 100 net markets, nearly all cited the ability to achieve a critical mass of buyers and sellers as *the* key success factor for their business. The A.T. Kearney research also stressed that deep industry knowledge is needed to build net markets correctly. That same industry knowledge will help companies choose the right ecosystems with which to align themselves—as we discussed in Chapter 3.

Within this same community of experts, there are a wide variety of theories on how to execute or apply the deep industry knowledge needed to reach critical mass, although to date, very little qualitative data has been collected to aid net markets in their quest to *reach* this critical mass. We think, however, that the secret to net market success today has changed little from the secrets of market success 10 years ago. The recipe for marketing leadership doesn't change in the course of a decade, even if the external market is radically different.

In *The Discipline of Market Leaders,* one of those books that was a business must-read in the 1990s (and not even written by us) author Michael Treacy extolled the goals of product innovation, operational excellence, and customer intimacy. He claimed that hot companies—including Intel, Schwab, Wal-Mart, and Southwest Airlines—got that way by choosing one of these "disciplines" and carrying it to almost religious fervor. Today, we have redefined these disciplines into what we call the 3Cs of B2B. These Cs are Content, Commerce, and Connection, and their relationship to their 1990s forebears is easily understood. Content is significant because innovation is as critical on a web site as it is in product development, commerce because low costs are still the key to operational excellence, and connection because customer intimacy is still critical. Unlike the 1990s, however, when Treacy claimed that market leaders could afford to rely on only *one* of these disciplines to reach market leadership, we believe—and the market is proving— that net markets need to excel in all three if they plan to survive the consolidation in net markets that is already under way.

It's generally agreed that the winners in the business-to-consumer (B2C) world are those that create stickiness— the eagerness of users to return to these sites with frequency. MediaMetrix compiles a list of B2C sites with the greatest usage in the United States, and the list is no sur-prise—is there anyone out there who by this time hasn't shopped at Amazon or surfed the categories of eBay? When A.T. Kearney analyzed the popularity of more than 100 B2C sites way back in the heady days of 1999, we found that the ones with the greatest stickiness were those that provided their viewers with content and connection. Moreover, despite the pre-IPO headlines of the Internet gold rush, web sites needed commerce as well—if they planned to make money, that is. The bottom line is that stickiness translates into brand equity and brand equity becomes market lead-ership. The relationship between stickiness, brand equity, and market leadership is just as clear in the B2B world— the only difference is that your customer is not your end user, but rather, resides further up the supply chain.

You can rank the net market you choose to participate in by how well it addresses each of the 3Cs. In this section we'll examine these critical factors in detail, and we'll define what can make the difference between a wishful and a successful market in the e-business world.

Chapter

Creating Stickiness with Content

"You can't sell from an empty cart," goes the seller's adage, and on the Internet, content is the only thing you can put in the cart: It's the pots and pans, it's the cart itself, and, frankly, it's the suit the seller wears.

At first glance, content—the relevant information included on the site—doesn't seem to resemble any sort of magic bullet. After all, if the commerce model is a good one, and if buyers and sellers are coming to the site, isn't information a bonus rather than a necessity? Experience, however, shows that content provides e-marketers with the opportunity to differentiate themselves and to build user loyalty. Content is the glue that creates that all-important stickiness in a web offering. Content charms the first-time visitor. It helps users understand how to get the most out of the site. It facilitates execution. Far from being nice but not necessary, content represents the hard part of what one e-marketer aptly described as "getting buyers and sellers to come to your site and to continue coming."

■ TYPES OF CONTENT

Content falls into three categories. The first is *community-building content,* which includes industry, advertising, and marketing information, supplier data, frequently asked questions (FAQs) about products and services, and it can include bulletin boards or other community input. The second is *commerce content,* which is data and documentation relating to the product or service being offered and can include such information as price, product description, and availability. The third is *office-work content,* which is the bureaucracy (in the best sense!) of the site.

➤ Community-Building Content

Net marketers recognize that an exchange is a human community, and community-building content is the human face on the machine. When industry participants and customers can access and exchange relevant, timely information, they naturally build a community. Once the community is created, it will continue to grow and build momentum. So managing net exchanges is not for the faint of heart: The hosting site no longer controls the community-building content but reaps the benefits of connecting companies, industries, associations, and the consumers who ultimately make purchasing decisions. Community-building content takes many forms, but divides pretty cleanly into static, or periodically updated, content (stuff we can manage) and dynamic, or user-created, content (stuff we can monitor).

Some static, or periodically updated, content provides information about the context of the web site and the products or services it provides. Site maps and pages devoted to FAQs are good examples. Other data reaches further out into the industry. Industry sector information of interest to users, such as periodic data and trade association updates, are often included. Other common features are job postings and recruitment insights; press releases; listings of seminars, shows, and training opportunities; and data on standards.

Dynamic, or user-created, content is harder to control but offers a valuable forum for users to interact. What better way to give participants what they want than to have them provide content themselves? Through bulletin boards, chat rooms, and feedback forums, participants can dynamically collaborate on ideas, ask questions, or vent.

A third category of community-building content consists of banner ads and hotlinks to other channel players, platform and application service providers, and ancillary service or content providers.

Developing a community-building content strategy is a difficult process: not enough, and the site dies from lack of interest; too much, and the users lose their way. The analogy to traditional marketing strategy is that community-building content is the brand strategy of the site: It's the emotional and intellectual environment that the user perceives, and comes to expect, from the exchange. As such, the aesthetic elements of the site are as critical an element of community-building content as the information on the site. It is a serious mistake to leave community-building content to the web-page designers and even worse to leave it to the technology people. Community-building content is fundamentally a marketing initiative, and it should be treated with the same diligence and care that Procter & Gamble dedicates to the launch of a major new product.

➤ Commerce Content

Whereas community-building content is the result of an effective brand strategy, rich commerce content is the result of an effective product design and development process. Commerce content is the functionality of the exchange product. Without commerce content, nothing happens. Rich commerce content helps educate both buyers and sellers, and it gives them greater control over the transaction process. As buyers gain more power through the transparency of pricing, product availability, and supplier sources, e-markets with the best overall commerce content will emerge as valued places for executing transactions. While the required commerce content varies by sector and transaction, common ingredients to exchange success include:

➤ *Product data.* Each of the hundreds of data fields that describe a product, a particular item, or its location falls into this category. Product data can be anything from general descriptions and part numbers that buyers can click and drop into their RFx or e-procurement processes, to highly detailed designs that engineers can click and drag onto their product development or packaging designs. This kind of commerce content is relatively static (or at least updated on a managed basis), but registration and synchronicity are critical to ensuring user satisfaction and trust.

Product data is organized by type into different product classifications. In the global market, several entities are involved in the classification of data, such as AC Nielson, Information Resources, Inc. (IRI), UDEX, and UNSPSC. Add the proprietary systems out there into the mix, and the global access of product data becomes quite limiting and cumbersome. The Global Commerce Initiative (GCI) is charged with defining a single product classification system as well as standard product attributes to create an openness in content.

➤ *Inventory data.* Inventory data falls into two measurement categories: Diachronic data (or flow information) measures inventory as it passes through the value chain; synchronic data (or stock information) measures inventory as it sits at points along the value chain. As net markets get better at managing inventory information, they are beginning to push the limit of their own version of the Heisenberg uncertainty principle, which states that you can't accurately measure an object's position and velocity at the same time. Many of the software solutions available to support supply-chain visibility solutions focus on one or the other, and a complementary fix needs to be put in place to get a sufficiently robust view of the value chain.

This kind of commerce content is hugely and necessarily dynamic—if it isn't dynamic it isn't useful. Once again, managing access authorization and subscription is critical—more on that later.

➤ *Pricing information.* Accuracy and synchronization are critical here, too, but more important is the absolute promise that competitors won't see each other's pricing. Most industries have many different price lists and pricing points for wholesale, retail, corporate, or bulk customers and volume purchases in many different regional or national markets in different currencies. So e-markets must assure buyers and sellers that they are getting the most accurate—meaning their own, current—pricing information and that their pricing isn't being shared with their competitors. Net markets also add value by presenting unbiased information to prospective customers who just want the facts, thank you, and would rather not be inundated by follow-up sales calls and price quotes. Pricing content is managed rather than dynamic.

➤ *Product-related information.* Net markets provide an almost unlimited range of valuable collateral information about products offered on the site, including technology reports, performance data, graphic images, specification requirements, and industry standards. Houstonstreet.com even provides weather updates on its site to aid traders in predicting energy needs and making purchases accordingly.

➤ *Company profiles and ratings.* In many industries, net markets are reshaping supply chains among hundreds of thousands or millions of buyers and sellers. While no one is likely to complain about having access to a slew of new partners, dealing with a supplier you've just met on the web is a nerve-wracking experience at best. Independent trading-community service providers like UCCnet will eventually offer pricing and availability of all registered suppliers, while affiliated e-markets may offer information that is oriented toward their channel partners. A note of caution: In the new economy, as in the old, market information is only as reliable and impartial as its source.

➤ *Transaction process management.* Net markets help buyers and sellers track purchases from initial bidding (e-RFx) to final delivery. Did you expect a huge shipment of packaging materials yesterday? Log on and see where it is. Access to information associated with the transaction—such as inspection data and postsale customer support—allows buyers and sellers to better manage the entire procurement process.

➤ *User purchase information.* Net markets can differentiate themselves through the types of information they provide about their customers' historical purchasing behavior. Data mining and data warehousing can be used to help users learn about products bought and sold, prices, and bidding histories; this information is particularly useful in analyzing trends and creating forecasts of future buying behavior. But with the opportunity comes a huge responsibility: Net markets must take extraordinary care not to breach the trust of their users.

➤ Office-Work Content

Michael Dertouzos from MIT (Massachusetts Institute of Technology) comments that while we like to think of content as being the same thing as intellectual property, in truth, 90 percent of content is office work: the e-mails, messages, processes, templates, forms, and files that lubricate the nuggets of intellectual property around the system to create value. For a net exchange, office-work content provides the context in which any activity takes place. Need to register? Need a password? Structure a document? Enter an auction? Send a message? Update a database? It all happens around office-work content. If community-building content is like a brand strategy, and commerce content is like product functionality, then office-work content is like the channel strategy: how to deliver the message and the product to the user in the best way possible. And "best" in this case certainly doesn't mean "most." As a matter of fact, transparency and ease of use are key drivers of user satisfaction. That's where standards come in.

Developing standards simplifies communication by allowing users to accurately predict what will be in a data field. Deep-layer standards, or business-process standards, simplify communication by permitting users to accurately predict what data fields will be included in a communication. Where deep-layer standards are not possible or not desired, protocols such as XML provide metamessaging techniques that introduce the data field at the same time the data is transmitted (see Chapter 12). The data wrapper information is an important part of office-work content.

■ CONTENT MANAGEMENT

Content may be king, but presenting quantities of data in a hard-to-navigate fashion merely creates dumpware. A simple rule applies: The more content on the site, the greater the need for an appropriate site-mapping capability. Remember the last time you visited a web site that took too long to produce images or that was too confusing to navigate? Chances are you got fed up and went on to another site. Using a web site should be logical and intuitive, not the cyber-equivalent of trying to solve the *New York Times*'s Sunday crossword puzzle. Although it sounds simple enough to transition a catalog or other data file from paper to electronic format, in practice it is difficult. To gain the most value, the information must be organized and categorized, integrated, and as dynamic as necessary.

Generally space is not an issue. Rather, the number of click-throughs required to get to the desired information is the key driver of user satisfaction or frustration. Therefore, descriptions should be as full and complete as needed to provide sufficient information to buyers. Content must be categorized and indexed to mirror the users' thinking. Access features such as "My Catalog" will allow buyers to customize the catalog and pull preferred products directly into their personalized page or to reshape the site map according to their own cognitive processes. In a recent survey conducted across a broad range of Internet sites, sites that have effective user-customization features enjoy 87 percent higher usage than similar sites that don't.

It goes without saying that content must be kept current, but this doesn't mean infinitely dynamic. Ski conditions sites generally update their web views once every 15 minutes—more dynamic doesn't add value. Regardless of the frequency of updates, or the dynamism of the data, managing content is a monstrous task. It is easy to get thousands of relevant pages on a site with any complexity, and each page has to be managed with the care and precision generally reserved for an important letter to your most important customer. As a result, there is a growing group of third-party content managers or providers whose value is the assurance of content with sufficient richness and validity. While some exchanges host the content themselves, others provide suppliers and buyers with the punch-out capability to access catalogs and then integrate or replicate the data through the net market environment. Some third-party providers are offering catalog maintenance services, catalog maintenance tools like those offered by Cardonet, and foundation architecture support to suppliers and buyers like that provided by UCCnet.

Content is the heart and soul of an exchange: It builds the community, it is the engine of growth, it gets things done. Without it, there is nothing. With too much of it, exchanges are crushed under their own weight. Everyone weighs in on content. Marketing mavens drive it as much as they drive brand strategy; engineers and product development gurus drive it as much as they drive product and service functionality; administrative experts drive it as much as they run your offices and drive your business processes. Lawyers, salesmen, merchants, human resources (HR), IT—all are essential to this important element of an exchange. Doing it right isn't just a nice idea; it's survival.

■ QUESTIONS

How much data is enough—but not too much? What would you want to see on a site that described your product or service? Where are the rat holes in your content (or, in current parlance, the "mink holes," which are rat holes that, although they feel good while you're in them, don't provide value to your effort)?

What data (such as regulatory information or industry results) would likely draw companies to a net market that serves your industry? What data would you want to be sure not to include because it would antagonize your visitors?

How do you know how well your pricing and other sensitive information is being safeguarded when you join a net market? Who is doing the protecting? Do you have a solid relationship with someone who views your security and confidentiality as being as important as you do?

Chapter

Follow the Money

Commerce Is Still Core
to E-Commerce

Let's talk money. How much should you pay to do business in a net market? Or—to get to the million-dollar question—how much is the market really worth to you? In this chapter, we look at different types of pricing models, discuss relationships between price and value, and explain why today's good answers should get thrown out the window tomorrow.

It's long been said that success and luck favor the prepared. In business, preparation is an outgrowth of vision and strategy. A.T. Kearney has developed a practical framework for developing e-business strategy, applying domain or industry knowledge, and successfully building participation in net markets. It centers on what we call the 3Cs of B2B: commerce, content, and connection; in this chapter we discuss commerce.

In the early days of e-commerce, all eyes were glued to that ubiquitous "e." "Let's focus on the technology and staking out our e-territory," the dot-com pioneers said. The financial rewards, they added, will roll in later. But when later came, the rewards were noticeably absent and red was the prevailing color of profit-and-loss (P&L) statements everywhere. Now the time has come for attention to return to the basics. The new view of e-commerce success echoes business school fundamentals: Forget the "e" of e-commerce and focus on the "commerce."

As we discussed in Chapter 2, there are a variety of net market models to choose from. The success or failure of any particular net market depends primarily on whether it can build liquidity. In fact, in an A.T. Kearney study of executives representing more than 100 net markets, nearly all cited the ability to achieve a critical mass of buyers and sellers as the key success factor for their business. The A.T. Kearney research also stressed that deep commercial knowledge of the industry sector is needed to build net markets correctly and to choose the right trading communities.

Our community of experts is as varied as their theories on how to execute or apply the deep industry knowledge needed to reach critical mass. They are not alone. Until recently, very little qualitative data has been collected to aid net markets in their quest to *reach* this critical mass.

But now that the dust of the early days has settled, several models of commerce have emerged that help net marketers develop that ever-critical critical mass. How they work and which one is right for your company are matters that depend on what you are marketing and who your customer is. In this chapter, we examine the basics of what you need to know to make this all-important decision.

■ CATALOG: ALL THE OPTIONS, ALL THE TIME

Although it sounds a little prosaic, an online catalog is the most powerful e-commerce model, and it frequently represents a first step for companies wanting to trade online. This is because so much preparatory work needs to be done to get a decent catalog online. A consumer example: Amazon.com is nothing more than a very well-put-together catalog. Online catalogs facilitate product comparisons, allow for customized presentations, and enable more rapid identification of preferred goods. The term *catalog,* however, tricks us into thinking that lots of these catalogs already exist—not so! In many sectors, information on less than 10 percent of available products is represented on electronic product information files accessible via the Internet.

The catalog solution can take advantage of one of two methodologies. First, catalogs enable (but do not require) online purchasing at predetermined prices. This solution largely makes money on transaction fees or margin, as it relies on large amounts of trading volume directly on the site. Netbuy.com, for example, sells electronic components in a multivendor catalog format. Second, catalogs facilitate offline negotiation of purchase price or availability. The e-market generally guarantees that the listed product is available for purchase at the list price. This strategy often involves a subscription or a posting fee, as net markets have little other leverage to ensure that the transaction is completed. Comps.com, for example, a commercial property e-market, helps match buyers and sellers by aggregating an extensive list of available commercial properties and then leaving it up to the respective parties to negotiate offline.

While a majority of catalog-solution providers charge transaction fees to suppliers, they also rely more heavily on listing, subscription, and advertising revenues than markets that use more dynamic trading models. Catalog solutions are popular in industries that sell chemical reagents, semiconductors and electronic components, and medical supplies. These industries share the following characteristics:

➤ *High product search costs.* All net markets cite the elimination of high search costs as a key benefit, and this is the primary inefficiency addressed by a catalog solution. Consider how much faster it is to buy from one source rather than leaf through several paper catalogs to compare features and prices. And for hard-to-find products, a few minutes on the Internet can accomplish far more than dozens of phone calls.

➤ *Little change in price.* Catalog solutions work best in industries where price volatility is low. Frequent price changes pose a maintenance nightmare. This is not an insurmountable problem, but fluctuating prices require more sophisticated approaches to managing synchronicity.

➤ *Time-critical purchasing.* Catalog solutions are extremely useful in industries where buyers and sellers can't afford the delay related to confirming the availability of products and services at an acceptable price. "Our business model relies on same-day or next-day delivery of auto parts," a tier-two supplier to the auto giants says. "Our buyers can't wait a week for the auction process to secure a part they need immediately."

➤ *Supply-chain breakdown.* The distribution chain isn't always perfect. Sometimes it fails even with supplier partners. When this happens, often a catalog aggregator can step in to fill the gap.

A catalog solution is not only a logical first step to online trading, it also provides its users some early wins— the kind of low-hanging fruit that is just waiting to be plucked. For one thing, these catalogs provide entrée to new markets without crossing traditional national borders. One committed member of the WorldWide Retail Exchange is also working with several small electronic catalogers in discrete markets. "We see them as a way to reach out to new markets, for instance, India and South America," the marketing executive explains.

Even if your company is not ready to commit to online purchasing, e-catalogs may be a way to hedge your bets and stay prepared to jump onboard in the future. That's the belief of Susan McKay, an executive at Aircast Inc., a medical products manufacturer in Summit, New Jersey. "Whatever your company, whatever your position today, you have to just get started doing transactions on the net. Who cares what percentage of your business it is now?" she asked an audience at the recent B2B Leadership Forum. Aircast does about 40 percent of its business via EDI, which probably means that the company won't transition that business to the Internet, at least not in the near term. Still, she says, "the big growth potential is online."

Where prices are volatile, a catalog solution is not the ideal long-term commerce mechanism, however, because it can take longer to record the price changes than the life expectancy of the prices. Think of stock prices. Buyers and suppliers in industries with such high price volatility are better off with a more dynamic trading model that allows for real-time pricing based on market conditions. Each of the three other trading mechanisms we'll describe—auction, hyperauction, and liquid exchange—is more dynamic and each offers unique benefits.

■ AUCTION: SEEK THE HIGHEST— OR LOWEST—BIDDER

Based solely on its ability to garner the best price, this commerce mechanism quickly gained popularity in the business-to-consumer space as well as at eBay and other consumer-to-consumer (C2C) sites. It has specific application in business-to-business as well, where price is determined through bids submitted on unique or individual offerings within a limited time frame—usually several hours, arranged with advance notice to all bidders.

Electronic auctions can favor buyer or seller. First, forward auctions work best when there is one seller and many buyers. An example is Autodaq, an e-business automotive company that provides the infrastructure and services to facilitate the trade of wholesale used cars on the Internet. Conversely, reverse auctions are ideal when there is one buyer and many sellers. Aerospan, the leading net market in the aviation industry, for example, offers reverse auctions in which one buyer sends out a request for parts (RFP) to all the member suppliers for everything, from propellers to oxygen masks (see Chapter 9).

Auction models generally favor the initiator of the request, at least in terms of price. Because of bidder competition, forward auctions typically yield sellers a higher price, while reverse auctions help would-be buyers find better deals. But participants can enjoy benefits as well as initiators. Buyers in regular auctions can access greater product or service selection and availability. Sellers in reverse auctions have access to more buyers—as well as the opportunity to bounce an established supplier who may not be as responsive in the new auction setting. This efficient market pricing of individual goods and services can occur where the following characteristics exist:

> *Unique items.* The auction model works well for products and services that are unique or at least definable and where value cannot easily be determined.

> *Price volatility.* Because single-parameter auctions focus solely on price, they flourish only where price volatility offers either the buyer or the seller an advantage. One high-tech marketer commented that auctions work well in a supply-constrained environment with volatile prices, "however, this is usually not the case with new IT equipment," he said.

> *Concentration of buyers and/or sellers.* Because an auction is fundamentally a one-to-many transaction, more than one bidder must be involved in order to drive price competition. Who initiates and who bids is often a function of the distribution of power in a particular supply chain.

➤ *Familiarity with the auction concept.* A virtual auction is easiest to implement in markets where commerce has traditionally been conducted in auction fashion. A net marketer who facilitates trades between auto dealers and providers observed, "Our model is important because dealers are accustomed to buying cars that way already." Note that the RFx process that most companies use to buy a broad range of direct and indirect items is structurally the same as auctions, only in slow motion—lasting weeks rather than a few hours.

➤ *New market opportunity.* Auctions may create a new market opportunity for a buyer or seller. For example, online markets promise to revolutionize the asset disposition industry by expanding the seller's reach globally while streamlining the historically inefficient process with assets that, as one net marketer says, "are usually written off by the seller anyway."

➤ *Purchasing that is not time-critical.* Time-critical parts will never be successfully sold via auctions. "Auctions are not a big part of our industry," one manufacturing firm told us. "There is too much time and risk involved when ordering for the production line." Although, as online marketing matures, manufacturing firms will probably buy long-lead parts—or elements of long-term contracts—via auctions, it is certainly true that most of the initial auctions are for indirect goods.

Despite its popularity in B2C situations, the auction model has some limitations for wide use in the B2B space. One net marketer calls auctions a "niche play applying only to certain markets. The end user does not have the time and patience always to go through the bidding process, and manufacturers need specific products with current dates." Furthermore, auctions are too price-centric for many B2B purchases. When other criteria, such as quality, vary among suppliers, auctions may not provide enough information in real time to enable bidders to determine true value or to mitigate risk. The current flurry of auction action will peak and diminish as more powerful offerings are developed.

■ HYPERAUCTION: FASTER IS BETTER

Already, auctions in B2B markets are evolving toward a souped-up, slimmed-down business model we call the hyperauction, which incorporates the benefits of offline purchasing with the efficiencies of online transactions. The hyperauction model speeds and automates the auction process by defining and standardizing the criteria that buyers may use in making their purchase decision, and it enables complex transactions based on those criteria to be completed automatically. Because the buyer predefines buying parameters, the bidder merely states his preferences up front. The net market software is set up to automatically search for the appropriate item or bundle of items, and to execute, bid, and close transactions, even without a human interface.

The hyperauction eliminates the human interaction in the actual bidding process, saving a substantial amount of time for buyers and sellers alike. It also simulates complex, real-life-buying procedures not possible in the standard auction format, including:

> ➤ *Multiparameter bidding.* Net markets set standard buying parameters such as quality rating, technical specifications or brand name, thus enabling participants to concentrate on variables that may be more critical to them than price.

> ➤ *Automated proxy bidding.* Complex contingencies can be built into the overall purchase of products, enabling bidders to buy on the terms they need. For

example, a buyer can execute a winning bid on an item contingent upon securing credit.

➤ *Bundling and unbundling capability.* Net markets can offer buyers the option to buy goods either together or separately, allowing bidders to obtain the best price for their combination of items.

Many e-marketers believe that the increased functionality of the hyperauction model will drive increased transaction volume through their sites. A net marketer in the metals industry stated, "We need to do this next level of auctioning in order to better meet our buyers' and sellers' needs."

Preplanning is key with hyperauctions. The model can automate negotiations and permit proxy bidding. Industries that adopt this model can speed their supply chains and focus on higher-value tasks. Other success factors in this model are similar to those inherent in an auction: Hyperauctions work best when buyers or sellers are fragmented and when participants are familiar with the auction concept. Moreover, as in auctions, a new market opportunity may be created.

The net market executives must be able to disaggregate a product description into well-defined parameters that represent the key buying decisions necessary to conduct automated, intelligent auctions. For instance, advertising is often bought and sold not by the type of magazine or TV show on which the ad will be shown, but by the type of readership or viewing audience the show attracts. If an advertising e-market can successfully define the parameters that influence the purchase of advertising—ratings, demographics, and frequency—it can allow buyers to make their advertising purchases automatically based on their specifications. Adauction.com, an advertising exchange, does this by utilizing Nielsen/Nat Ratings data.

Similarly, the more complex the supply chain, the greater the need for the features that hyperauctions can provide. That's because hyperauctions can mimic the contingencies, product bundling, multiple buying criteria and real-time execution inherent in real life buying—a tremendous benefit to complex supply chains. Creditex.com, for example, is a financial services e-market that allows its participants to engage in trading credit-risk derivatives—a tremendously complex process.

Because of its potential, hyperauctions are already emerging in disparate industries including transportation, advertising, printing, steel, and financial services. The primary disadvantage of this commerce model is that if liquidity is limited, purchasing will not be completed in real time. The more parameters that are placed on a trade, the fewer suppliers will be available to fulfill them. Fewer suppliers inevitably cuts into price competition and lengthens the bidding process. However, hyperauctions that can draw a critical mass of buyers and sellers may achieve the necessary liquidity to move to the most advanced dynamic trading model that has yet emerged—the liquid exchange.

■ LIQUID EXCHANGE: NOBODY DOES IT BETTER

A liquid exchange is a many-to-many Nasdaq-like exchange that allows multiple buyers and sellers to trade in real time with all exchange participants. All requests are filled quickly, prices are transparent—perhaps available on a computer screen or electronic ticker—and purchases are virtually guaranteed with the promise of quick fulfillment of mission-critical products and services. Immense liquidity is a requirement and a result of transparent pricing and a guaranteed supply of product to meet purchase requirements. This far-reaching model merges the benefits of dynamic trading with the promise of rapidly fulfilling mission-critical products and services.

Liquid exchanges can create financial instruments to allow buyers and sellers to manage risk in their supply chains. The value of this is enormous to all participants, particularly in capital-intensive industries. The market also benefits directly, usually through greater transaction volume (and transaction fees) due to the participation of traders and speculators who may or may not ultimately consume or add value to the product. The best current examples of liquid exchanges are the existing equity exchanges, with the continuing modifications they are making to become fully net-ready.

The main distinction between a hyperauction and a liquid exchange is that the latter takes place in a real-time trading environment in which participants can trade at will with little risk in either securing or selling the product at the published price. But liquidity is not guaranteed. A super-sized market player that can drive a lot of business to the site would have little incentive to do so. "As probably the largest buyer of a single grade of resin, why would I give up my company's competitive advantage?" one marketer asked. Moreover, if too many parameters are used to define the product or service, the number of qualified suppliers—and liquidity—diminishes.

This model will only emerge in select industries, due to the combination of characteristics required for its success. Prices must be volatile, buyers and/or sellers fragmented and substitutable to a certain degree, product parameters defined and standardized, participants familiar (and comfortable) with dynamic trading, and new market opportunities created.

Because prices are transparent in the liquid exchange, this model provides both a true market price and allows for immediate purchase of goods. So items with high price volatility that are bought for immediate use—which can range from goods such as wholesale natural gas to broadband services—work well on liquid exchanges. Time-critical goods may not be appropriate for this method, depending upon the delivery mechanism, but in industries such as telecommunications and energy, quick delivery can be arranged and executed digitally, and liquidity assured. The greatest risk is that the volatile nature of the spot market may result in transactions being completed at higher-than-desired prices, but this risk can be mitigated through limit-order capabilities.

Frequently-traded goods are more likely to move to a liquid exchange than those traded on a longer-term contact basis. Thus, the outlook for agribusiness net markets, including FoodUSA, WorldOfFruit, and Gofish, is promising due to high trading frequency, perishability of the goods, and time-critical purchasing requirements.

Whether it's the simple bulletin board, catalog form, or the more complex liquid exchange, exchange organizers choosing the commerce system that best fits their industry characteristics and needs will have the greatest chance to achieve critical mass. New market entrants at this point will be facing a number of challenges when choosing their models. In the beginning, it was all about finding customers, avoiding regulatory slip-ups, and making money on the transaction. Already, however, the market is changing. It's quickly moving to a point where buyer-seller discovery and commodity pricing in certain areas—for example, bulk chemicals—will render early models ineffective. Strategists have to look more closely at how to handle the back end and how to add value through streamlining business processes. That leads to a quick progression from models that add little value and minimal information to the more complex systems.

■ THE RIGHT VALUE

What is your value proposition to your customers—the unique worth of your product or service? Do you have the highest quality consumer electronics around? The cheapest, most practical line of casual clothing? We've found in our client work that senior executives often *think* they know their value proposition, but throw them in a room with their peers, and they discover that their visions of exactly what the company has to offer are subtly, but importantly, different. Similarly, when a group of formidable competitors gets together, they will often identify the same things that give them their unique competitiveness. Be sure your management team is in full agreement on the value you offer. Involvement in net markets is a perfect occasion, if not the cause, for such awareness.

Which brings us to the next issue: How will the e-market you are evaluating (or creating) help you give your customers what you've promised? Net markets can offer a variety of benefits, from lower transaction costs to better demand forecasting to faster time to market. If your value proposition centers on offering new and innovative products, an e-market that helps you collaborate with key partners and design gadgets more quickly offers you value that is better aligned with your strategy than an e-market that focuses on transaction costs.

Consider the experience at TeleCentric, a B2B service provider to the telecommunications industry. CEO and cofounder Gary Slagel clearly understood the concept of value to his customers. Highly inefficient business processes characterized the industry, and in his dealings with potential customers, he heard their message loud and clear: They wanted a seamless flow of information and efficient value-chain management. They also wanted transparency that would allow them to identify engineering and delivery problems in advance.

This goal, unfortunately, is notoriously difficult to achieve. The suggestion was made to provide a simpler solution that would be easy to implement, but Slagel knew that might fall short of what his customers really valued. His persistence paid off in the end, when he partnered with i2, Ariba, and others to provide collaborative procurement and supply-chain management functionalities. By focusing on what customers really needed rather than chasing the

current fad, TeleCentric built itself a reputation as a partner that brings differentiated value to its customers.

It is easy to be seduced by a net market's bells and whis-
tles and technological savvy. However, as we've said, it's not
about the technology, but how the technology can put you
at the head of the pack. When you pay for fancy, gee-whiz
features that net you nothing in the end, you dilute the
value you receive.

Here's the bottom line. Investors expect a net market to
offer value that is 5 to 10 times the cost; that's a good bench-
mark for you, too. Net markets that price too high won't
lure enough participants to gain liquidity. Those that price
too low leave money on the table. ForRetail.com, for example, was forced to change its pricing strategy, for charging
a transaction fee of 5 percent was not enough to create sufficient revenues. As a result, the company removed itself
from being a net market to becoming an applications service provider—an increasingly common route for troubled
net markets. In the long run, you need the net market to
achieve liquidity and want it to be healthy financially as
much as the investors do. Another way to look at it is this:
If the net market offers you true value and prices correctly,
you will be at a competitive disadvantage if you don't join.

If you are establishing or evaluating a net market that
remains in the developmental or early stages, opportunity
is knocking at your door. Insert yourself into the process of
determining services and products to be offered. Press for
what will offer you value, rather than what's easy or already
on the agenda. Whether you are a participant or simply an
investor, your input will be valued.

■ SORTING THROUGH
TRANSACTION TYPES

Net markets have a variety of pricing strategies and mechanisms for implementing them. As you evaluate a net mar-

ket in terms of price, consider not only the fee structure for your type of participant (e.g., buyer, supplier distributor), but also how others are charged. These are the most common models:

➤ *Transaction fees.* Charging for each completed deal remains the most popular model—for now. An A.T. Kearney survey in 2000 found that 87 percent of net markets charged transaction fees (three-quarters of them charged the seller only—and it's likely that for most other cases, the buyer pushed back the charge to the seller). As with other pricing models, the concept can be adapted to meet the needs of the particular e-market and its customers; the fee can be a flat one or it can vary based on transaction size, volume pushed through the system, or other criteria. Where the benefits of participating in a net market are sufficiently higher than these transaction costs, the model works. However, the practice of charging by the deal will not hold up over time as the value a net market offers shifts. One participant in our survey told us, "Transaction fees will be the majority initially, but we expect them to go down to 20 percent of the mix over time. The other 80 percent will be value-added services such as logistics and credit clearing."

➤ *Subscription or membership fees.* Some e-markets may charge their members an annual fee. The membership fee can be the same for all who join, although this may deter smaller companies or any party that feels it gets less bang for its buck than others. It can vary based on the value proposition, perhaps with an upper limit, and it can increase or decrease as volume increases, depending on the net market's needs and corresponding strategy.

➤ *Markup.* The net market maker acts much like a reseller and charges for the cost plus an additional percentage. This is particularly relevant for ASP models, in which the net market really operates as buying consortium for technology. GlobalNet-Xchange (GNX), for example, acts as Oracle's oracle for its few large, independent members—or CPG-markets, spear-headed by Nestlé and Danone, which seems little more than a SAP-sapper.

➤ *Fees for value-added services.* This concept, which is expected to gain in popularity, is based on charging customers for services related to the transaction, such as financial services, logistics, or consulting. These value-added services are seen to be the primary benefit of the future of participating in net markets.

■ QUESTIONS

What are the key components of your organization's value proposition? What functions offered by an exchange would provide the greatest value to you?

Across the supply chain, what are the sources of buyer and supplier power in your industry?

What are characteristics of the types of goods and services your company trades in? For example, do they tend to be commodity-type goods or are they highly specific and differentiated?

Are there new potential markets your organization could enter as the result of access to a world market?

What factors associated with your company or industry lend themselves to the various types of auction formats? Would any of these models add value by addressing pain points, or general inefficiencies, in your supply chain?

Chapter

Connection

Can We Talk?

Connection involves more than connecting the dot(com)s. In addition to connecting with other sites, this third C also includes the issues of connecting participants socially and establishing connections across the entire value chain. Power Players that effectively analyze and understand how to connect all the necessary information up and down the value chain will enjoy a defendable competitive advantage—because they will have defined the value chains that own them.

Companies frequently find that one of the surprising benefits of net market participation is access to a better platform on which to build internal integration and communication models. Just as Y2K provided the boardroom push to update systems behind the firewall, today, B2B is providing the impetus to create seamless connections across the web—and will also renovate the technology behind the firewall.

Particularly for those multidivisional companies that have built up their business through acquisitions over the years (and what e-market Power Player hasn't?), using Internet-based utilities and net market formats can smooth over the hodge-podge of operating systems that they typically support. Similarly, for global companies that have developed specific systems for their regional or national markets, net markets can provide an impetus to standard-ize data communication and business process standards. This helps these firms substantially streamline operations in their smaller markets (think Thailand and Argentina), and take advantage of synergies offered by aggregating volume or more diversified operations.

Not surprisingly, many net market Power Players don't realize the need for this transparency until they join a B2B. Then, experience becomes an unforgiving teacher. In the old paradigm, if they had trouble exploiting the Internet utility, their first response would be to fix the problem behind their own firewall and then offer a handshake to the net market. But today, once they do a sharp-edged analysis of this solution, most quickly realize that using the Internet utility to level their internal playing field is generally a better option both in terms of time and development expense.

It's a little-known fact, but we have discovered that many leading Power Players are championing their involvement in net markets not only to improve their home office operations or processes with their biggest suppliers or biggest customers, but to help bring less-developed divisions and markets up to best practices quickly, and to help the small- and medium-sized enterprises with which they work to get to a level of efficiency and intimacy enjoyed in their best-developed relationships.

■ WALK, DON'T RUN

New e-markets tend to develop according to a certain pre-scribed format. During the first phase of development, the primary focus of the founders is typically to get the site up and running as quickly as possible, get some PR going, and enable information exchange among value-chain partners.

Only after those goals are achieved do e-market executives typically turn their attention to the much more long-term challenges of integrating the various systems among their member companies so they can communicate, transact business online with transparency, and share the necessary data to complete the transaction. Only then do the horrors of legacy systems, incomplete ERP investments and short-sighted knowledge management come to the fore.

We may be living in the twenty-first century, but it is clear that many net markets are going online with flashy web pages but almost medieval back-end functionality. As a result, the spiffy electronic procurement form you e-mail to your supplier could spit out as a fax that is hand-carried around the warehouse to be fulfilled. Clearly, this Band-Aid approach does not promise success. Instead, net markets need to take the time to identify the parties they need to connect with—and determine the technology they will use to make these connections. We subdivide connection into three types:

➤ *Intraconnection.* Internal processes between the buyer and seller in the transaction.

➤ *Interconnection.* Connecting other supply-chain participants involved in the transaction.

➤ *Extraconnection.* Extending the supply chain to other net markets.

Whoever you are connecting with, the connections have to be transparent, seamless, and effort-free.

➤ Intraconnection: Net Market Success Starts at Home

At its most basic level, data exchange occurs between the buyers and sellers in the e-transaction. The RFP is set out, the bid is accepted, then executed and confirmed, and the net market enables the trade to be settled automatically— or with minimal human interaction—from order to payment to delivery.

Thus, when a buyer selects the goods or accepts the bid, the payment system automatically accounts for the payable. On the seller side, when the bid is accepted and the goods are committed, an accounts receivable entry can be made. Note that the timing of the financial flows is a matter of negotiation between buyer and seller. On the one hand, buyers can finance sellers' operations (think own-brand fashion apparel); on the other hand, sellers can finance buyers' operations (think scan-based trading). It's simple in concept—the difficulties reside in the connections.

These actions require integrating capabilities between the buyer's and seller's ERP and other legacy systems. Companies such as SeeBeyond and webMethods have built annual revenue streams of $500 million in this connector space. We'll delve into the ramifications of legacy systems further in Chapter 12.

➤ Interconnection: Supply Chains Will Dominate

Automatic connections between buyer and seller are just the beginning. Already, net markets are increasing the functionality of their applications in response to their members' demands. Customers are demanding end-to-end solutions, and e-markets are responding by partnering with third-party service providers and linking with others up and down the value chain.

Log on to an asset disposition site, for example, and you will not only find a buyer for your sunseted equipment but you will also be able to obtain financing for the product, delivery services, and insurance to cover the transaction. Venture capitalist Ray Lane of Kleiner Perkins Caulfield & Byers predicted recently, "Supply chains of the future will 'own' the companies, not vice versa. Down the road, companies will be asking, 'What's my role in that supply chain? What do I bring to it?'" Certainly, as we already discussed in Chapter 3, the smart companies will be those that own the points where value is created along the value chain.

Most net markets recognize the need to align themselves with other markets and providers to create the kind of end-to-end solutions they believe will be necessary to attract customers and achieve differentiation in the future. Yet, we're still in the early days of net markets, and only a few have so far turned to successfully address this issue. New companies such as Arzoon, Metreo, and Supply Solutions depend on the cross-the-firewall connection; we have also seen tremendous growth in companies such as Archive, webMethods, and SeeBeyond.com that enable this connection.

Ventro, an early e–poster child, was one of the first vertical-exchange operators to launch new platforms that combine transaction-based with service-based offerings. It now has several divisions, one of which operates in almost 60 vertical markets; another operates high-volume exchanges for third parties. There's also an offshoot called VN Solutions that provides a range of end-to-end technical solutions for market makers. And Ventro's not finished yet: Ultimately it may sell off its owned vertical markets in favor of a new market service provider model. How quickly we morph!

➤ Extraconnection: Exchange to Exchange

Member companies want more, more, more. To be successful over time, we anticipate that net markets will need to make and implement *all* the necessary connections for their industry. The drive toward new levels of collaboration and the sense that in any market there are some problems that simply cannot be addressed by a single market maker is pushing exchanges to seek partnerships beyond existing competencies.

Here's a Power Play that illustrates the concept: Honeywell, United Technologies and B.F. Goodrich launched MyAircraft in February 2000 to deliver aftermarket parts and services to transport, passenger, and military carriers. Six months later, MyAircraft.com announced that it would merge with AirNewco, an exchange founded as a supply chain by a potpourri of leading airlines just a few months previously.

The new venture, now rechristened Cordiem, will service buyers and sellers with a selection of product and services offerings—online catalogs, reverse and forward auctions, inventory and supply-chain management tools, and transaction support features. The combined venture will be managed separately from its two constituent exchanges, while ownership will be shared between MyAircraft.com and the members of the airline-backed exchange. Industry observers see the move as a way to embrace more suppliers, who now will not need to plug into two or more separate exchanges to obtain products and services.

Then there's PartMiner, with its expertise in creating liquidity around shortages of electronic components through spot transaction. It has partnered with E2open, the electronics e-marketplace made up of industry heavyweights IBM, Hitachi, Lucent, Nortel, Matsushita, and Toshiba, in a classic match of buyer scale and a great sourcing base.

In perhaps the mother of all Power Plays, Transora, the consumer packaged-goods behemoth whose investors include 50 of the industry's largest companies, entered into exchange-to-exchange agreements with Novopoint and Foodtrader. The deals will integrate the services of these not-insignificant B2Bs into Transora's hub. Rich Kauffeld, Transora's chief alliance officer, called Novopoint and Foodtrader "natural choices because they are leading the development of Internet marketplaces for ingredient suppliers to consumer goods manufacturers." And Transora CEO Judy Sprieser believes that "these alliances will accelerate adoption of Internet marketplace services among industry companies and bring the economic benefits of the Internet to the industry more quickly. We expect to quickly engage in similar arrangements with leading e-marketplaces in other service areas of importance to our participants."

These moves extend the trend of collaboration that naturally develops among exchange members beyond their own sphere to the sphere of affiliated exchanges. The alliances that created both Transora and the WorldWide Retail Exchange were a direct response to Wal-Mart's superstore retailing megastatus on the one hand, the inequitable structure of GNX on the other hand and the fear of being nibbled to death by the dot-com ducks on the third—new technologies challenge us to have more than two hands. Clearly, the race for scale will continue.

■ IF YOU CAN'T SEE IT, IT MUST BE THERE

We haven't talked about technology in this discussion on connection, and there's a good reason: If you notice the technology, then there is a problem with it. After all, when connection works well, it's because the technology is transparent. Even in this era of rapidly developing bandwidth, exchanges still outstrip the capacity of technology to deliver. Suffice it to say that whatever we write in this book about how much technology capacity you need or how much your customers expect, our numbers will quickly be out-of-date—the quantity will grow exponentially over time.

From a strategic point of view, our recommendation is to treat technology infrastructure like capital: Make sure you have rapid access to a scalable quantity, and invest underutilized resources wisely. And remember that your weighted average cost of technology is higher than the hardware and software costs—don't forget that infrastructure, maintenance, training, and administration don't come cheap.

■ QUESTIONS

What are some of the industries with which your potential exchange could partner? In other words, where do natural synergies exist in your value chain? As they used to say in the industrial-equipment sector in the 1980s, "Look to the left, look to the right, next year two of you will be gone." The difference is that now there will be some alien sitting next to you next year.

Is your organization currently dealing with internal IT compatibility problems resulting from the integration of new acquisitions or just plain deferred investment? Do you have far-flung international divisions for which Internet access to a company-standard approach to your business would improve their performance perhaps 10 or 15 percent along some key performance indicators?

Have your dealings with small- and medium-sized enterprises been constrained by administrative difficulties? Do you periodically pare down the left-hand tail of your supply base, knowing that you may be losing nuance and sophistication in your suppliers? Is your company required to promote sourcing from companies owned by targeted ethnic, regional, or gender groups? Does instant "level playing field" sound good?

III Part

How the Leaders Are Playing the Game

Today's best-in-class organizations got that way by being smart. It didn't take the Power Players long to learn their lessons from dot-com mania and to muscle in on the web, demonstrating both power and agility in their actions. The big boys first struck back in force in early 2000, when groups of key industry players got tired of reading *Wall Street Journal* articles about how the newbies were stealing the market share they appropriately thought was theirs. In numerous industries, market leaders came together in amazingly short order to substantially returf the playing field and hopefully to reclaim that market capitalization.

Armed with the human capital needed to run an organization and the know-how and experience that comes from previous business expansions, and freed from the need either to build a brand name or to convince venture capitalists to buy into their plans, the Power Players quickly succeeded in trashing the Nasdaq and its global equivalents. In so doing, however, their own market capitalization did not correspondingly change. That's because the business path forward now more clearly depends on the ability to implement than the ability to strike a deal.

Each story of an e-marketplace set up by Power Players shows how they are moving forward in their sector—not only to develop and deploy technologies that are innovative and sustainable but also to deal with the difficult issues of crafting an extended enterprise to fulfill the promise of the Internet without running foul of the commissions or dissipating their own company's competitive advantage. You may not be a Big Three automaker, but their experiences will show what *your* company will need to do in order to participate fully in these Power Plays or what you can expect if you should prefer to go it alone.

Let's set the stage. Imagine a room full of senior executives from large, hugely conservative, highly successful, and sometimes competitive companies. They've come together to launch a cooperative market venture. Each firm is putting up millions of dollars (generally 1 to 12 million) to fund the enterprise. They all agree to collaborate through shared knowledge, strategies, and resources for the mutually acceptable purpose of regaining competitive advantage from their biggest competitor (read, Wal-Mart, Barnes & Noble, or any other category-killer you love to hate).

Even more powerful, once their market is up and running, these founding companies will turn altruistic by allowing other interested companies to join their club and enjoy the same membership privileges. There's more: They have every reason to believe that the FTC and other antimonopoly watchdogs give thumbs-up to the venture's charter.

Is this a trip to Fantasy Island? Not at all. This scenario describes the formula for the way truly open net markets have been formed. Variations of the electronic exchange are numerous, of course, and we will present and describe several real net market configurations so that you may analyze for yourself the relevant advantages and disadvantages of each, and how well each fits the strategic needs of your company.

These net markets described in detail in this section were chosen both for their industry breadth and their value propositions. In addition, we'll share insights and firsthand experiences from the founding members and executives of each exchange. Welcome to a tour through:

➤ *WorldWide Retail Exchange.* They've got the consumers—who wants to play?

➤ *Covisint.* Big things happen when the Big Three get
together.

➤ *Aerospan.* This air transport market has the clout of
a longtime industry organization.

The dot-com start-ups may have blazed the path to business on the Internet by showing the value of content and
community offerings—but they forgot that the business of
business is making money. The Power Players with their
own powerful content and commerce clout are now on the
stage: Let's move on to some of today's best new organizations, which have taken e-business to the next level by using
scale and savvy to develop and further exploit business on
the web.

Chapter

Being the Biggest from Birth

The WorldWide Retail Exchange

The WorldWide Retail Exchange was conceived and born at Internet speed. In a few weeks the founders—on both sides of the Atlantic and around the world—pulled together to respond to what they felt were biased net market solutions to create a truly open net market solution for the biggest market in the world.

It all started in early 2000 when CVS/pharmacy, the American drugstore chain, made plans to establish its own presence online. At first, company executives considered joining the then-existing GlobalNetXchange (GNX) e-market, but "we decided GNX was set up to help the people who were the founders, not those who came later," explains corporate executive Dave Rickard. "So we decided to join with some other retailers and start our own exchange." What came next happened in a matter of weeks.

Why the rush? The alternative—the cost of doing nothing—was very clear, says Claude Palmieri of Auchan, the French retailer and another founder in the WorldWide Retail Exchange (WWRE). The mistakes Palmieri had seen in earlier B2B exchange efforts, coupled with a keen sense of where e-commerce might be heading, led him to decide that the time was ripe for Auchan to take a leadership position in an open exchange.

"Everyone moved fast," he says. "Senior executives from U.S. firms immediately reached out to European retailers who were thinking along the same lines. We held virtual meetings over the phone lines, and collectively green-lighted a global $500 billion commercial net market idea in two weeks."

When U.K.-based Kingfisher got the call from the core group in the United States, David Jobson recounts, "We did a crude cost/benefit analysis. It was a no-brainer for us, being in at the outset, rubbing shoulders with peers around the world." In fact, he says, "our CEO, who is typically very cautious, took to the idea of participating almost spontaneously."

Thus, the WorldWide Retail Exchange was born. With one old-fashioned stroke of the pen, a 17-member network was set up that was more than twice the size of Wal-Mart.

■ REALIZING THE RAISON D'ÊTRE

Members of the WorldWide Retail Exchange—food, general merchandise, textile, and drugstore companies—participate in a full range of e-commerce transactions with their vendors, either in conjunction with or independently of one another. Each retailer uses the WWRE to build or supplement its own infrastructure and to plan and execute business all along the value chain.

The issue that led Dave Rickard and CVS to action in the very beginning—the belief that an exchange should be open and that the benefits should accrue to all participants, not just the founders—remains a central principle of the World-Wide Retail Exchange. As a result, no favoritism is asked or given. Of course, volume breaks are offered, but equally to all, so the price for any given service is the same whether you're a big company or a small one—what matters is how you use the exchange. In fact, the WWRE is set up as a not-for-profit organization: The URL for it even ends in .org, not the .com standard for a for-profit corporation. Instead of an IPO to make the founders rich, all the benefits are pushed along, as they are accrued, to the members.

The WWRE seeks to revolutionize trading relationships and to do the following:

➤ Create open systems in which firms can form short- or long-term relationships with one or many partners

➤ Bring new buyer and seller opportunities to its trading partners

➤ Provide an electronic interface that lowers transaction costs for both buyer and seller

➤ Create transparency to the marketplace that eliminates the costs of maintaining hedges and sandbags in the value chain

➤ Rapidly develop new e-commerce business models and implement advanced technologies

In addition, the WorldWide Retail Exchange creates value for its participants across the entire value chain by developing a frictionless and transparent market to exchange goods and services. Transactions are conducted from end to end along the supply chain—from sourcing through settlement.

And that's not all. Participants will continue to benefit down the road, as new services are phased in, through use of new software tools for more efficient e-procurement, new product development, vendor certification, supply chain management, and shared-services outsourcing. In the future, the WWRE will offer retailers tailored state-of-the-art technology solutions as they are evaluated and approved by the WWRE.

■ A TEAM OF TITANS

Sheer volume easily made the WWRE the largest retail exchange the day the paperwork was signed. It reached aggregate revenues of approximately $750 billion by the end of 2000, and an additional 36 companies joined the original 17, bringing the membership total to 53. By comparison, the GlobalNetXchange had revenues of $195 billion, and Wal-Mart, so recently the retail gorilla, has fallen to number three with revenues of $165 billion. In phase two of digital commerce, size and scale matter.

In fact, it is fair to say that the David-and-Goliath battles of early e-commerce days have been replaced by battles between similarly sized e-titans. Auchan's Palmieri thinks that this is a model most people don't consider. It's much more common to "think of the industry paradigm of going from *scale to speed*," he says, "but many don't think of the Internet paradigm of going from *speed to scale*. That's the more strategic issue," he insists.

Start-up capital for the WWRE has come from the founding members, who committed to fund it through its development phase until it was cash-flow positive. For most of these global members, that investment is a small price to pay to lower their own transaction costs throughout the industry, although many executives active in the WWRE also see their role in an almost evangelical light. They are proud to be working with their counterparts across the industry to make the playing field more efficient—and competitive—for everyone.

Still, the potential for significant savings undoubtedly contributes to their enthusiasm. Conducting business through the WWRE is estimated to generate savings of 3.2 percent of revenue. That's heady news in an industry where one-tenth of one percentage point of cost can justify a megamerger. Where will the savings come from? Retailers expect to pocket benefits at multiple points along the value chain, and many of the savings are well known. The availability of Internet technology and the development of global standards, however, accelerate the ability of retailers to capture those benefits.

Savings will come from a variety of areas:

➤ Reduced acquisition costs and improved asset productivity in the sourcing cycle

➤ Fresher product and better sell-through because of a better product-development cycle

➤ Asset productivity and reduced reclaim due to collaborative planning, forecasting, and replenishment

➤ Reduced inventories and better asset utilization from improved e-procurement

➤ Better assortments and happier customers through better category management

➤ Reduced administrative costs because each person in the organization becomes more productive using Internet technology to execute his or her duties

In the five-to-seven-year rollout, the more relevant question is "Where won't they find savings?"

There is also a sequencing of savings. In the early months, much of the savings will come from aggregated volumes and use of reverse auctions to craft new supply market solutions. In midcourse, integration will unlock benefits as sandbags and hedges in the value chain dissolve and as costs for retailers as well as suppliers find a new—lower—equilibrium. Over the longer term, collaboration enabled by technology and standards will allow value-chain partners to work together and pool inventory information, manage production against total value-chain inventories, really sell to the scanner, and fulfill much of the vision of efficient consumer response (ECR) that has been rattling around the industry for the past decade.

In the long term, the WorldWide Retail Exchange will operate as a not-for-profit (but not-for-loss) company, providing technology and commercial services to participating companies. Founding members will recover their initial investment with a set interest rate, and once that occurs, all participants will enjoy cost savings based on their use of the WWRE's offerings.

■ IS BIGGER ALWAYS BETTER?

The WWRE hadn't planned on having 17 founding members—interest just grew very quickly. The number was in some ways unwieldy. "We were at a point with 17 members [on the board] where books would tell you we were too large," recalls CVS's Rickard. And still more retailers wanted on board.

What to do? Representatives of those 17 companies are members of the board, and new members are also represented. "But today we have an executive committee of the board, which is smaller and workable in the long term," Rickard explains. "We can work issues in a group of ten."

Many suppliers have also expressed an interest in becoming WWRE members, and at time of publication the WWRE is considering how to best serve these so-called dogs in the kingdom of cats. To date, suppliers participate on advisory boards in which their views are incorporated into policies and procedures are developed. In the longer run, it will likely become even clearer that the goals of suppliers and retailers truly are the same.

Suppliers benefit in many ways:

➤ Communication with WWRE members can take place via any Internet browser without any specially configured software.

➤ Transparency in demand for products and services allows suppliers to adjust inventories and orders accordingly.

➤ Market exposure will increase via the addition of previously unreachable new buyers.

➤ Participants gain access to a state-of-the-art communications platform for collaborative planning, forecasting, and replenishment (CPFR) and supply-chain management.

➤ Collaboration on new product development and commercialization will improve.

➤ Production capacity can be better managed due to value-chain visibility.

In the short run, costs go down. In the long run, assets go away. It was going to happen anyway, they said. With Power Play exchanges, it's going to happen a lot faster.

■ WHAT MAKES THIS EXCHANGE A WINNER?

There are several exchanges serving the food and retail markets today. The GlobalNetXchange and Transora, to name just two, were set up at the same time as the WorldWide Retail Exchange, also with considerable corporate backing. However, WWRE members are adamant that their exchange offers a superior—and ultimately more sustainable—business model.

The WorldWide Retail Exchange is open, neutral, jointly managed, and driven by the needs and goals of its participating retailers. It does not represent technology in search of a market, and it has chosen and aligned with IT providers based solely on their solutions—not preexisting relationships with members. And, as mentioned earlier, because it is a not-for-profit organization, equity in the WWRE flows through to participants, and there are no plans for an IPO.

In terms of governance, the WorldWide Retail Exchange consists of four development boards representing the interests of members in specific vertical industry segments—food, drug, textiles, and general merchandise.

Recognizing that this new model of exchange needed to foster a collaborative mind-set, the founders hammered out key principles to support their unified vision for success. These principles are more than words on paper—they reflect a common mind-set and understanding of the WWRE. "To my mind, the reason the WWRE works better than GNX is that the founders share a vision and we know what we stand for and what we will do and what we won't do," says Dave Rickard of CVS. "Once we got a common vision, then keeping the group moving in the right direction has been a fairly simple task."

The principles are:

> ➤ *The exchange is open.* It is set up so that no company can gain a proprietary advantage over another based on that company's composition or the length of time the company has been involved with the exchange.

> ➤ *The exchange will use the best technology.* "We are not tied to any technology provider," the principles read; no technology company has an ownership position in the exchange. "We interview technology leaders and they compete for this business. We will choose the technology that is the best today, and most important, we will have the freedom to change technologies in the future if warranted."

> ➤ *The goal of the WWRE is to use the Internet to lower costs and improve efficiency in the retail marketplace.* "While the exchange will be a separate, neutral company, we are not looking to make a profit on a future IPO of its stock."

> ➤ *The exchange will be established as a neutral company with independent management.* None of the top exchange executives came from member companies: Colin Dyer, CEO, came from a successful stint as CEO at Courtaulds; Don Norman, CIO, is a household name in retail technology implementation; Robert Heaton,

CFO, came from a run in retail industry and financial consulting; and Peter Jueptner, CCO, most recently ran two of Campbell's multibillion-dollar businesses. Solid businessmen all, but beholden to none.

➤ *All retailers will participate with the same fee structure.* It can be a sliding scale based on transaction volume, but big and small, founding member or occasional user, retailer or supplier, all play on the same level field.

➤ *Confidentiality of transactions is critical.* "Private information will remain private," the principles read.

■ WHERE THE BUCK STOPS

Colin Dyer became the first chief executive officer of the WWRE in September 2000. Previously, Dyer was the chief executive of Courtaulds Textiles, a clothing and fabric company operating in 17 countries and employing more than 20,000 people, until Sara Lee acquired Courtaulds. He manages a growing staff of global technical, functional, and retail specialists. Staffing is always a challenge in these things, but in the meantime, he can tap into "a well of talent." He explains, "The commitment of the members and their generosity in committing people to our business is truly impressive. The challenge is to harness that talent to develop our products and services."

Dyer also maintains that, despite starting up during a full-employment economy, he has no trouble hiring the people he is seeking. And, he looks for more than retail experience. "I need flexibility, the ability to create structure in a non-structured environment," he says, "people who are critical, internationally minded and able to operate proactively."

For people who are excited at the prospect of breaking new ground, the exchange offers numerous challenges. It's not business-as-usual at the WorldWide Retail Exchange. "We have no models," Dyer warns. "We need to make it up as we go along. But all operational issues are solvable," he continues. "The biggest issues we face are figuring out how to adapt the ways in which large retailers and their suppliers interact. Our success in doing that will determine the way the WWRE will grow over the next few years."

Smaller issues, such as fixed office space and phone lines, have had to wait their turn. For the first months of life, the WWRE had been meeting in hotel rooms and borrowed space. But at the beginning of 2001, Dyer and his team set up shop in Alexandria, Virginia, in purpose-built facilities that accommodate the large, regular member meetings, as well as frequent, three- or four-point video-conferences around the globe.

Even though it is fair to say that the WWRE is still in its start-up phase, many of its members are highly experienced in e-commerce through their B2C and other B2B ventures. For example, Ahold (Netherlands) holds a 51 percent ownership in U.S.-based Internet grocer Peapod. J.C. Penney conducted more than $100 million in Internet sales in 2000 and expects to reach the $1 billion mark by 2003. Tesco is currently the world's largest Internet grocery delivery service with over 500,000 users and $200 million in sales, and Kmart has a major B2C presence with BlueLight.com.

Some of the members are involved in other B2B exchanges as well. David Jobson of Kingfisher says the U.K.-based consumer electronics, home improvement, and general merchandise company "had already started working with several other net markets including Global Sources in Hong Kong" when it joined the WorldWide Retail Exchange. The Hong Kong–based exchange offered capabilities "to help us reach out to new markets in India and South America." Kingfisher will continue to be involved with Global Sources, Jobson says, but he adds, "I can't see why we would want to be involved in any other major exchange if we can shape the WWRE correctly."

■ SEARCHING FOR WORLD-CLASS GOLD

Because a goal of the exchange is to bring the best technology possible to the table, it is not tied to any single technology provider. According to Albertson's executive vice president of technology, Pat Steele, the exchange signed a multiyear contract in September 2000 naming the B2B alliance triumvirate of IBM, i2, and Ariba as its preferred technology partner "on the basis of the breadth, scope and depth of the capabilities it has shown it can bring to bear on our requirements, its proven ability to implement solutions quickly and by acting as a unified entity in responding to our issues and needs during the selection process."

However, technology providers are interchangeable, and to ensure that flexibility, the WWRE is adopting universal standards. Albertson's Pat Steele sums up the issue succinctly: "As business moves to real-time interaction, standardization is critical. You must be sure that your data is absolutely standard. Otherwise the whole thing collapses." The exchange is supporting CPFR guidelines developed by the Voluntary Interindustry Commerce Standards (VICS) Association, as well as leading the development of emerging XML and Internet standards.

"Standards and standardization make much more sense in the WWRE setting," says Delhaize's Michel Eeckhout. "Our company has always been involved with standards and standards bodies such as the International Organization for Standardization [which promotes ISO 9000], but it was a regional [European] issue." The WWRE will encourage the development of standards that are open, voluntary, and evolving. It supports GCI but remains independent of those bodies for idea generation and pilots.

Security is maintained through proven best-of-breed technology, process control, and data firewalls. The data integrity and privacy of all participants in the WWRE is a paramount concern. Because of its role in creating cooperation among competitors, the WWRE determined that private information will stay private.

There is nothing like the power of an idea whose time has come. Once the realization hit in early 2000 that the revenue potential and savings opportunity in B2B vastly exceeded B2C commerce, the whole concept of commercial exchanges seemed to explode.

In the food and retail industries, the exchanges turned into land grabs both in breadth of content and geographic reach. In February 2000, Albertson's believed the exchange idea made sense but wondered how they were going to go it alone. Meanwhile, CVS wanted in—but didn't like any of the existing models already in the market. Pat Steele remembers that, "The vendors [IBM, Oracle, and others] and consultants came to us and said 'you need to take a look at this.'" But Steele felt that many companies were starting exchanges for the wrong reason, "which was to get to IPO and make money on the Internet."

As Steele recalls, Albertson's, CVS, Safeway, and Kmart had a better idea. "Collectively, companies coming together could fund a very expensive proposition that would end up being relatively inexpensive." At the same time, in Europe, Ahold, Delhaize, Tesco, and Auchan were developing similar ideas. The power of many would allow these companies to have industry clout and the wherewithal to move the industry forward and set the standards. "It was as if the stars were aligned because we really came together in about two weeks. A week later we had most of the European contingent on board, and a week after that we had an exchange," Steele continues. "I've never seen anything like it in my life."

In conversation with the founding executives, the unified purpose of the WWRE shines through. "Everybody's dedicated to the end game, process improvement and taking costs out, where the money can be made for this industry." In the technology area Steele adds that it's "one of the quickest, although not painless, ways to get the Internet inside your company, a lot faster than we would have otherwise done by ourselves." He is also very positive about the globalization opportunities. "The exchange gives participants a global perspective and helps them understand issues from a global point of view and proves access to global suppliers."

Minus a crystal ball, it's not possible to foretell the future of the WorldWide Retail Exchange. But, as John Gleeson of Walgreens states, one thing is clear: "We have so many big companies working on this that there is no doubt in my mind that we are going to succeed. We have scale and commitment."

■ QUESTIONS

What is the right balance of industry insiders and independent outsiders needed in a net market to produce the best results for your industry sector? Is such a net market developing? Can you accelerate its growth?

Does your industry's net market have a key set of principles and a unified vision? If not, what principles would you want to ensure are included?

What functions within your organization would likely be most affected by an exchange? Would your underlying concepts about competitive advantage change? Would the value of your currently perceived core competencies diminish or increase with your more active participation in a net market?

Chapter

Covisint Puts the Pedal to the Metal

In the midst of all the dot-com euphoria, a groundbreaking venture emerged that could very well rev up a sputtering Internet marketplace in the years ahead—particularly in the B2B arena. After all, anything that brings the highly competitive Big Three U.S. automakers to the same table is notable, and this time it proved to be more than just another high-level meeting of senior executives politely applauding Power Point slides. This time the result was Covisint.

On February 25, 2000, Ford Motor Company, General Motors, and DaimlerChrysler made history when they announced plans to fund the development of an independent company designed to harness the power of the Internet for streamlined purchasing, supply chain management and product development. Named Covisint—derived from *co* (for communication), *vis* (for vision) and *int* (for integration)—this web-based trade exchange was trumpeted as the next wave for B2B commerce.

The announcement raised many an eyebrow. But the venture grew even more newsworthy just two months later when Nissan of Japan and Renault of France said they were joining the Covisint venture. The *int* in Covisint quickly added a new dimension—international.

Reaction was—and in some cases still is—mixed. Some analysts proclaimed that Covisint would become the world's largest Internet marketplace, eventually handling an estimated $750 billion a year in purchases by automakers and suppliers. Others were skeptical, claiming that the venture's strategy remained unclear. Was Covisint striving to be a procurement specialist or a supply chain optimizer?

Dan Jankowski, a Covisint spokesperson, admitted that Covisint's communication of its mission suffered in the early days. "There was some confusion at the beginning," he noted, "and it was mostly our fault."

Despite the hoopla surrounding Covisint's birth, Jankowski was succinct in describing its ultimate goal: "The whole idea behind Covisint is to drive down costs and eliminate waste out of a system that is 100 years old."

■ SLOW TRAVEL THROUGH GOVERNMENT ROADBLOCKS

A strategic mission, to be sure, but not everyone was convinced after the announcement, particularly the U.S. and German governments. Both the U.S. Federal Trade Commission and the German Bundeskartellamt (Federal Cartel Office) immediately questioned whether Covisint was nothing more than a smokescreen that automakers could hide behind to strong-arm suppliers into their way of doing business. Such scrutiny and necessary approvals slowed Covisint's momentum in early 2000, but it emerged from the investigations unscathed.

On September 11, the FTC gave a bureaucratic thumbs-up; the Bundeskartellamt agreed on September 26. Each regulatory body, however, offered similar assessments. Although Covisint did not appear to be violating antitrust laws, both governing bodies insisted that they would keep their eyes on the venture as it developed.

With governmental roadblocks cleared, Covisint's founders put the pedal to the metal and moved from a planning organization to a Delaware-based limited liability corporation (LLC) in early December. Technology partners Oracle and Commerce One also came on board the multimember joint venture.

Working out of temporary headquarters in Southfield, Michigan, and European offices in Stuttgart, Germany, Covisint LLC has quite a to-do list for 2001. In April, Kevin English came on board as CEO. The net market is in the midst of hiring some 300 full-time employees to replace those currently on loan from the member organizations. In addition to setting up permanent offices in the U.S. and Europe, Covisint also plans to open locations in Asia. It has elected 12 of 17 members to its board of directors, including members from four of the five automaking partners. Other board appointments so far include CEOs and other senior executives from Delphi Automotive Systems, Johnson Controls, Siemens, Lear Corporation, and Magna International.

Although the to-do list has gotten shorter, the matter of a long-absent CEO is troubling. It took one full year after Covisint came into being to select the right leader. Such a lengthy search raised the volume of the Greek chorus: If speed is a defining characteristic of success in the age of "e," then this is hardly an encouraging sign.

Still, the powers-that-be have been quick to mount their defense. Addressing a panel at a conference in New York in December 2000, then acting CEO Rico Digirolamo spoke to the heart of the matter in selecting the right person to head this who's who of auto industry titans. "It's important for these exchanges to be seen to be independent. For Covisint, part of this process is trying to find someone not from one of the three major auto manufacturers who can lead this organization. This is hard work. We are looking for a '12' out of a '10' kind of individual." Digirolamo's job wasn't easy either. He followed interim CEO Alan Turfe, who left in July 2000 to become CEO of MetalSpectrum. Perhaps the job will get easier as latest reports suggest that Toyota, Mazda, Honda, and Mitsubishi, as well as Denso, a parts manufacturer with ties to Toyota, will soon be on board.

■ FROM 0 TO 60 IN NOTHING FLAT

Covisint's founders are adamant in their belief that the true value of e-business reaches the core of any business, resulting in more efficient, cost-effective, and flexible operations. As Jankowski explained, Covisint's overall tools and services focus on a key strategic goal—to put the industry on a fast track for progress while reducing inventory costs for its suppliers.

"Technology moves very fast, but the automotive industry moves at dinosaur speed," he added. "If we can reduce vehicle development time, which typically runs 24 to 48 months, to 12 to 18 months, then the automakers can respond faster to changing consumer tastes and make the industry more competitive." Covisint's marketing tagline, "Accelerating the Pace of Business," drives that point home.

In addition to speeding up vehicle development time, Covisint also envisions an online environment that will support original equipment manufacturers and suppliers in achieving the following goals:

➤ *Compressed order-to-delivery cycles.* The *co* part of Covisint, communication by way of the Internet, should speed up the long road from bubble-up to job one and minimize wasted effort.

➤ *Increased shareholder value within the automotive industry.* Because Covisint is an investment of industry Power Players, sector savings and equity appreciation flow to the parties that exploit Covisint most effectively.

➤ *Greater asset efficiency and utilization.* A more effective use of resources is a natural fallout of reduced cycle times. Perhaps the most valuable asset to be freed up is human intellectual capacity.

➤ *Higher profitability with direct impact to the bottom line.* Reduced transaction costs and costs of acquisition probably account for only 30 percent of the total benefits that Covisint users will enjoy. Once the full impact of the Covisint functionality and Internet capability is worked through the participating companies (a 7-to-10-year process), the value chain will have more profit in it as a percentage of costs. Whether it keeps this profitability or passes it along to the consumer is a strategic marketing decision.

➤ *More integrated supply-chain planning.* Beyond delivering the benefits of a compressed order-to-delivery cycle, Covisint has the potential to take integration through to production jobs and downstream logistics.

➤ *Reduced business process variability.* Eliminating needless variation has been a goal of the automotive sector for decades. Covisint gives participating companies a powerful new tool to push them a few sigmas closer to perfection.

Indeed, Covisint strives to differentiate itself from other existing e-business ventures that the company claims generally involve web-based services that focus on isolated tasks. Rather than offer incremental solutions that address the needs of isolated areas of a company, Covisint touts its blueprint as offering a more comprehensive and integrated product that can redesign the entire enterprise from enhanced product development through procurement and supply-chain management.

Extensive experience in and knowledge of the auto industry are key selling points for Covisint, according to Jankowski, and they are characteristics that will hopefully keep Covisint from following so many others into dot-gone land.

"Covisint is populated by a team of people who have incredible depth and knowledge of the automotive industry," he stated. "Our knowledge base is a differentiating factor."

■ TRANSPARENT VIRTUAL COLLABORATION

One of the most important enabling technologies Covisint brings to participants is the ability to collaborate from different places at different times, not only within the participant company, but up and down the value chain. Through Covisint Collaboration, a virtual project workspace for multienterprise product development teams, all teams can interact, share project-specific data, and conduct virtual meetings within a secure environment. The technology features real-time task tracking, visual collaboration tools, application sharing, and a multimedia notebook that captures discussions for decision management, knowledge sharing, and even crisis management.

Using the ipTeam platform developed by NexPrise Inc. with enhanced Internet-enabled three-dimensional imaging provided by e-Vis from Engineering Animation Inc., Covisint's Release 1.0 suite of products will move virtual collaboration beyond an individual organization and expand the reach across geographically diverse locations, multiple organizations, and even supply chains. Think of it as a supercharged form of videoconferencing and program tracking combined.

Jankowski explained that Covisint Collaboration will allow users to embrace virtual collaboration beyond its own infrastructure. "This type of product development can be done without Covisint within a single company," he noted. "But companies are hard-pressed right now to work in any real-time environment with other companies. With Covisint, however, it doesn't matter where everyone is because they can all see the same images and data at the same time, making changes and markups."

Such real-time development translates to bottom-line effectiveness, according to Jankowski. "Time is money, and the ability to eliminate the time needed to make decisions directly impacts the bottom line," in addition to reducing or eliminating costs associated with travel and document processing. Even more, Covisint believes these applications will support its mission of achieving faster time to market.

Then, in March 2001, Covisint announced plans to build a collaborative design portal to include collaborative product development, a definite increase in the depth of its current online, transaction-oriented quotation process. Jankowski told a conference group hosted by the Massachusetts-based Giga Information Group that Covisint's new portal is going to trim vehicle development times by nearly 60 percent, from 42 months down to 12 to 18 months. In the process, Covisint will cut about $3.5 million in paper-based costs from the design process.

■ THE POWER OF KNOWLEDGE

Covisint is developing a wide array of information services. Becoming a single information portal for the automotive industry, however, means more than aggregating third-party information providers—although Covisint will provide one-stop access to both general industry and company-specific information in a secure environment, including:

➤ Reference information on markets, market trends, demographics, and sales

➤ Long-term forecasts on automotive production

➤ Reports on consumer perceptions and consumption of final products

➤ Up-to-date regulatory information provided by OEMs and other industry sources

➤ Directories of end items and services providers, as well as third-party reviews of supply chain participants

But the exchange understands that as the design complexity of a product increases, so does the need for access to expert resources regarding unique technologies. Such expertise can come from within and without, and manufacturers and suppliers alike may be called upon to share their knowledge across the entire product development spectrum.

To that end, Covisint is launching a host of services, including:

➤ Product-development training and consulting

➤ An online library of material specifications

➤ Secure access to advanced technological developments

➤ A repository for design and other related information concerning reusable components and objects

➤ Automatic messaging to alert users based on their profiles and preferences

Once again, these services are aimed at boosting the bottom line via reductions in costs associated with technology acquisition and related skills and resources, while increasing the reuse of proven designs.

■ A GLOBAL MARKETPLACE

More effective procurement practices are another goal of the consortium. The auto industry's traditionally hierarchical and bureaucratic nature often translates into paper-intensive procurement processes that force procurement professionals to spend too much time on procedures. With Covisint, a variety of services are being designed to eliminate such costly functions and allow users to focus more on procurement strategies and improving supplier performance.

Covisint Quote Management—a suite of tools that handle document management, interenterprise management, and collaborative bidding—will provide electronic support for more efficient handling of RFQ and strategic sourcing. In addition, financial services, catalogs, and procurement links will be imbedded within the Covisint environment.

Auctions also will play a major role in the procurement functions and actually represent Covisint's first online ventures. ArvinMeritor Inc. was the first company to transact business on Covisint in early October 2000 when it piloted a live auction to buy injection molding on the exchange.

Jankowski affirms that auctions were the quickest means to show Covisint's potential while it was still very much under construction. "We focused on the auction method first because we knew what we could do," he added. "But we recognized that auctions alone could not carry the weight of a new company that would have a big impact on the industry."

Industry reports claim Covisint has concluded $1 billion in transactions already.

While designed to save money for its members and users, Covisint does plan to gain revenue through transaction fees that were not yet made public at the time we went to press. Several industry reports have indicated that Covisint has an IPO in the works for 2001; Jankowski would neither confirm nor deny the company's plans.

What is crucial to Covisint's financial success is the ability to attract a large number of the 20,000 suppliers involved with the auto industry. In December 2000, the company announced that more than 250 suppliers on two continents were already using its catalogs, auctions, and quote management and collaborative design tools. And it hopes to have more than 2,000 suppliers signed up by the end of 2001.

Covisint's success depends not just on the participation of tier-one suppliers, but the ability of these companies to exploit Covisint's functionality to shape their relationships with tier-two and tier-three suppliers, thereby generating a significant amount of business to create the liquidity required. Most financial analysts agree.

Several industry experts, however, believe that Covisint may have a tough time attracting the number of suppliers the exchange needs to be liquid and profitable, given that some suppliers are still wary that the B2B exchange could, in fact, drive down their own margins. A number of supplier-based exchanges have launched on the Internet that could keep many from signing up as they wait to see which ones get the most traction and establish themselves as e-marketplace forces.

Others note that Covisint's decision to offer key suppliers profit sharing rather than an ownership stake in the company has made it less attractive. *Automotive News* quoted one anonymous executive from a tier-one supplier as saying that the current profit sharing arrangement would result in discounted fees charged to suppliers but only when Covisint meets its minimum profitability level.

■ READING THE ROAD SIGNS AHEAD

Jankowski freely acknowledges that Covisint faces many challenges in the future, particularly regarding suppliers' fears and perceptions. "We are not a puppet of the manufacturers," Jankowski stated. "We are industry focused, not company focused."

He was also quick to point out that every founding member of the board retains a minority stake in the company. "Covisint wasn't started for the sake of the founders," he noted. "We've made the organization independent of the automakers."

Although not committing to a future IPO, Jankowski said the Covisint culture is based on that mentality. "We have an IPO mentality, which means that everyone in Covisint has only the Covisint mission on its mind."

Ultimately, success for Covisint will lie in its ability to show the supplier community that it means business for everyone involved. "The supplier community will not trust what we say, only what we do," Jankowski said. "They focus on deeds, not words."

■ QUESTIONS

When all the major competitors of an industry come together to create an e-marketplace, how do you ensure that the collaboration does not break down? How can you ensure that it ramps up as quickly as possible? What can your company do to speed up the process?

In an industry moving toward such online collaboration between the Power Players, how does a smaller firm compete and survive? What steps should small- and medium-sized companies take to be ready, on the one hand, and to represent the class, on the other?

Chapter

Moving Essential Parts around the World the Aerospan Way

Willie Sutton liked to rob banks because, he said, "that's where the money is." That was then. Today, the e-commerce band-wagon is flying high—with well over 1,000 online business marketplaces inviting your trade in 2000 and AMR Research projecting $580 billion in transacted business by year-end 2001. So where's all the loot? So far it's been elusive to all but a few players, such as software companies, which have carved out valuable niches using the old '49ers pick-and-shovel approach, supplying tools needed by all participants in online marketplaces.

Air transport exhibits all the right characteristics for a successful online exchange opportunity. Picture an industry in which 100 percent performance is expected every time and in which 99.9 percent is just not tolerable. You've just gotta love it. Regulation may have officially gone away from the U.S. airline industry in the late 1970s, but the amount of documentation and traceability that's required for an aircraft part would give comfort to the pickiest of nitpick-ers. To repeat, you've just gotta love it. Unless, of course, you are the one saddled with doing all of the compliance work. However, there are no arguments here from us executives who are frequent flyers. So bring on the safeguards.

Now let's get a better look at the operating picture in air transport. The top-tier players are controlling most of the market, but there are many more small-to-medium-size outfits and some tier-two players as well. There's a huge industry spend (well over $100 billion total spend and nearly $3 billion of that just in aftermarket parts for aircraft); an inefficient supply chain where most of the business is still done offline with faxes, phones, and e-mails; a fragmented customer base; and a highly information-driven purchasing process. In short, there are a lot of market inefficiencies that we'll talk about in this chapter. One big one is inventory.

"When we did the feasibility study in early 1999, we identified about $57 billion in inventory being held by the airlines," recalls Hal Chrisman, who now serves as Aerospan's marketing and business-development honcho. "About $15 billion of that is consumed every year. That's a .25× turnover rate [based on the nearly $60 billion currently held inventory]. In most any other industry, that's completely unacceptable." Why does such an inventory problem exist? Chrisman ticks off two important reasons: First, the OEMs like to play it safe and tend to overprovision the airlines. Second, and more important, airline station managers are trained to have a just-in-case rather than just-in-time mentality. It's a recognized fact in the management business that what gets measured gets done, and airline managers are measured on dispatch reliability, not on the amount of inventory they are holding. Simply put, the consequences of holding a plane on the ground are more noticeable than the cost of holding inventory. However, Chrisman believes an opportunity exists to conservatively optimize 20 to 30 percent of that spend, and eventually as much as 50 percent. Even splitting the difference between the two numerical goals yields a potential reduction of around $20 billion in inventory. That's more than enough fiscal opportunity to launch an e-business venture. But there's more to the story.

In air transport, the procurement process is detailed. Take a typical airline buyer's day, circa 1999: The buyer needs a certain number of parts. First, the buyer gets a stack of parts requests and prioritizes them based on value. Because there are typically more parts requests than can be sourced in a given day, eventually the buyer will place orders for the balance with either the supplier that was used the last time or an OEM. For the sourced parts, the buyer requests information from various suppliers. The supplier typically goes to the shop or warehouse and pulls the traceability paperwork (e.g., an FAA 8130), which is normally held with the part and is specific to the life of that one part, and photocopies it. After returning the original documentation to the part it came from, the supplier phones or faxes the document to the buyer. The buyer looks over the papers, makes a decision about, for example, parts number 1, 3, 5, and 7 on the list—deeming them acceptable based on personal criteria such as how many hours are left on limited-life parts—and tosses out the documents for the unwanted parts. Now the negotiation begins. The buyer contacts the seller about the parts of interest and then it's how much, how soon, and a number of back and forths by phone or fax. But remember: Isn't "e" supposed to eliminate this paperwork and the to-ing and fro-ing? This is, after all, a slow and primitive way to do business—especially when there are a lot of items on the shopping list.

That was the situation back in spring 1999, when the whole idea of B2B marketplaces was a fuzzy bogie on the radar screen. Later that year, SITA, the air transport industry group, and AAR, the aftermarket air transport supplier, got together for a meeting in Chicago. Their goal? To take the online commerce idea and start developing the technology side so it would become a marketable product. Based on some very conservative assumptions, they projected a business that would be profitable in its third year.

Armed with that data, the two organizations made the decision to launch. Aerospan was born.

While all this was happening in late 1999, the idea of Power Players coming together at a single conference table was still counterintuitive. No one had heard of Covisint. Charles Withrow, Aerospan's director of business development, recalls a meeting in the later part of January with Delta, and it was just that, a meeting with Delta. "We weren't thinking, *do you want to bring six other airlines along?* In less than a year, we had changed our thinking." At the time, that was the way it was done; nascent markets were getting people on board one company at a time. The consortia idea came later.

What's the first-mover advantage to be a pioneer in the air transport space? Withrow responds that it lasts "less than 90 days." He believes Aerospan to be "the first company in the air transport space to set up an Internet-based online exchange." Although there had been other online listing services, such as Partsbase and ILS, Aerospan was the first that enabled transactions.

■ WINGS AROUND THE WORLD

Sometimes nothing succeeds like serendipity. However, it usually favors the prepared. Simply put, you have to be an innovator to recognize and to be ready to seize an opportunistic series of events.

SITA is a neutral industry organization—a cooperative partnership owned by its many member airlines plus a few suppliers including powerhouses Airbus and Boeing. SITA is a major player in the technological area through its ownership of the world's largest global telecommunications network connecting airlines and airports worldwide. In 1997, in association with Morgan Stanley Dean Witter, it created a for-profit telecom venture called Equant. With that deal, part of the company became publicly owned and part continued to be owned by SITA members. By the end of 1999, SITA began to think about selling Equant's network, which was finally sold to France Telecom in 2001, generating a multibillion-dollar war chest for SITA and heavenly windfall profits for some of its members. Flush with the proceeds of the Equant offering, SITA was ready to look for other businesses in which to invest. The organization realized that its future would be different from the past, and it needed a new business to operate. In fact, it had already created SITA Inc. to pursue potential new investments.

The positioning idea was enjoying clear skies. In just a few months, SITA and AAR put up $5 million each to create the Aerospan product. Withrow remembers that the start-up's strategy was to be a buyercentric, supplier-friendly electronic marketplace. "We clearly saw that the airlines were our customers. We were going to build an application the airlines would find tailored to their needs from a purchasing standpoint and they'd be able to source in the aftermarket, not just from the aftermarket supplier, but the OEMs as well. We wanted to make it easy for the OEMs to have a channel for their customers to order from them using traditional or new means." Traditional ordering meant the EDI standard used in the industry (known as Spec 2000), which allowed customers to purchase aftermarket supplies from any source, aftermarket supplier, or OEM. "We always saw the initial pitch going to the airlines and then later the suppliers."

Attracting suppliers is a little easier in air transport than, for example, retail. There are only a limited number of possibilities. Inventory is expensive. Aviation buyers enjoy some leverage but nothing like the velvet hammer that Wal-Mart holds over its retail suppliers. Nevertheless, the reality played out differently than the theory. First, the unexpected happened. As Michel Saunier, Aerospan's president and chief technology officer relates, "Despite our belief that SITA was acting on behalf of the airline industry (and its shareholders), two industry consortia were announced in May 2000 that forced Aerospan to rethink its focus." The original business plan had addressed a total industry spend exceeding $100 billion. But when AirNewco and Aeroxchange made their move that May, these two ventures took most of the industry spend off the table and froze the market. Despite the setback, Aerospan boldly launched shortly thereafter, and went live in September 2000 with, among others, a beta customer that was also an AirNewco customer. "It's not rocket science," Withrow declares. "You have a plan and then suddenly most of the spend is taken off the table. To go forward, you have to project capturing a much larger share of a smaller market."

That crisis was scarcely over when Aerospan's suppliers balked. The problem was simple: As long as AAR was a major equity partner in Aerospan, suppliers wouldn't play. "AAR was a competitor to many of the suppliers that we were asking to participate in the marketplace, and as an owner in the exchange it was hard to convince them that there wouldn't be any preferential treatment," recalls Chrisman. Surely they could be persuaded that AAR wouldn't have any access to their data? "True, but it came down to money. You couldn't convince them that it was a good idea to participate in something that was going to put money in the pocket of their biggest competitor. As 2000 closed, AAR sold its shares to SITA, which is now Aerospan's sole parent. Also by that time, Duncan Alexander had joined Aerospan as its CEO.

■ EITHER ON THE BUS OR OFF THE BUS

Aerospan is a key offering in SITA's e-business portfolio. Under the leadership of Jean-Marc Bouvier, who is driving the development of the company's e-business portfolio, SITA's focus is clearly on value-chain management and developing end-to-end integrated offerings for its members to pass along to their customers. These value chains are truly the soup-to-nuts of air transport and include:

➤ The traveler's journey from reservations and ticketing and check-in and boarding to flight and baggage handling

➤ Door-to-door delivery of air freight from carrier selection, pickup and loading, and transport to unloading and delivery

➤ Aircraft lifecycle management from planning and designing, building, and monitoring and maintaining to disposition

Bouvier makes clear that technology is not the only component of change. "The air transport community is going through a massive restructuring," he says. "The starting point is business process and emerging business models that are made possible by Internet-related technologies. Technology is only an enabler for this transformation."

Initially, the Aerospan development team focused on the commerce capabilities of the exchange. After researching what was available in off-the-shelf procurement platforms and given the unique inventory model, documentation needs, and requirements-based buying mandated for the air transport industry, the core technology team decided early that it would have to custom-build a transaction engine to meet its performance standards. In addition, the group knew that speed to market was absolutely critical. The team decided that the risk was just too great to go with an off-the-shelf product and rework a custom-built solution on top of it sufficient for their one-of-a-kind industry needs. In the end, they were concerned they might find that it wasn't going to do the right job or that the core off-the-shelf platform was not sufficient. Saunier feels that the team made the right choice at the time, but that today some off-the-shelf products exist that could probably have changed the decision. However, he confirms that to date, thanks to this decision, Aerospan is in a great position to integrate a realm of new functionality and value-added services that competitors will have a tough time beating.

Their commerce capabilities filled the development team's days, but Aerospan did not ignore either content or community. Aerospan purchased content-management software and also recruited a team to focus on what to do with the content infrastructure that would go there. Working simultaneously, the technology team focused on content enablement. This parallel effort paid off well as the e-market was able to build a very robust transaction engine with solid content-management capabilities. Community, of course, was part of Aerospan's value proposition from the e-market's inception. And since getting up and running, Aerospan has signed numerous deals to bring industry and community information to members. These include job postings, a press room of industry news, and conference and expo information.

■ THE VIEW FROM 30,000 FEET

Aerospan is a pioneering innovator, and has been nurtured by Power Players with a solid grounding in the high-flying world of air transport. Catching up with Duncan Alexander, we found a charismatic CEO and industry veteran confident that he and his experienced management team can keep Aerospan flying through the current turbulence in the markets and on to clear skies ahead. No launch aborts here.

"There will be a shakeout," Alexander prophesied. "Winners will be driven by the airlines or somebody who has managed to really create value." That value, Alexander clearly believes, will be determined by the robustness—or lack thereof—of the offerings: "What some people claim is an e-marketplace now is just a listing service. We've got a marketplace where buyers and sellers can come together on a screen. When a buyer does something, a seller sees it, and vice versa. That's a lot different than going to an inventory listing and sending someone an e-mail. This is an aggregation of many to many [buyers and sellers] in a value chain. The endgame will be driven by the buyers [not the OEMs] as they are the fee-paying customers."

What about those suppliers that decide to balk? "They may be resistant to e-markets but it's inevitable," according to Alexander. "They can't be Luddites," he continues, because Luddites tend to disappear. He finds an analogy with the travel industry: "First Priceline came along and then the airlines started offering seats directly to consumers. The [pundits] said that the Internet would bring an end to travel agencies." In actuality, travel agencies that have embraced the Internet have expanded their business reach.

As for parts suppliers, "Any sacrifice they may make on the margins due to the price and availability transparency will be offset by the gains they make in planning, forecasting and replenishment." Alexander believes that this is the next stage of value in e-marketplaces. The endgame here is automatic replenishment of parts that are necessary to keep needed levels of supply in inventory, and not one piece more. "No more just-in-case stock that ties up capital needlessly," he said. "The real-time e-marketplace will create a market for excess or surplus inventory, by moving it from the warehouse of one supplier who has too much of it to another who has too little or to a new group of buyers who formerly couldn't be reached without the global network of the exchange." Of course, all this will take time. Meanwhile, Aerospan's job is to ensure that its offerings are robust and seamless. The goal is to develop real-time inventory processing. But Aerospan isn't flying into altogether unfamiliar territory; again, Alexander sees a connection to an earlier paradigm shift in the travel industry, and that was the development of global distribution systems under the trade names of Sabre, Worldspan, and Galileo.

Think about it, Alexander said: "You, as a traveler and buyer, can get direct access to American Airlines' seat inventory and in real time purchase a seat and debit it from their supply. It's a capability we take for granted—and it's available 24/7 with all the airlines." Alexander continues, "What's happening in our industry is the same. You'll need a year-old part; you'll buy it off a live inventory list. And everything that happens around that—the financial settlement, the tracking of the goods, the final delivery of the item and electronic ticketing of the part—will happen electronically." That's the e-marketplace at work. "We talked about these kinds of changes 10 years ago and today the technology exists to do it," Alexander said.

The other area where the e-marketplace will make a difference is supply-chain management. Because e-markets will aggregate buyers and sellers, supply-chain management will become visible to everyone on the supply chain. Thus, when a part is debited from inventory, the buyer may own a new propeller, but the buyer is not the only one who is affected. The regional manufacturer then shifts more propellers to the warehouse, and the need for more propellers ricochets up the value chain all the way to raw-parts delivery. "This will all take time," Alexander continued. "What we have accomplished so far is to bring together buyers and sellers to do commerce. The next step will evolve into an ERP update and integration—no matter what back-office systems the various companies have. This will, in turn, integrate into an improved supply chain."

One of the nonnegotiable rules of air transport is that when a part is needed, it is needed *now*. And it is needed wherever the aircraft happens to be. Here is where an e-market can provide the intelligence to get the right part to the right place. Let's say, for example, that the airline needs an emergency chute for a Boeing 777 in Sweden. The airline needs it now, because the chute was accidentally hit and deployed and damaged. Until the chute is replaced, that aircraft is grounded, and so are all the passengers that have to get from here to there. Not to mention the crew.

Today, the airline would have several buyers in a back office laboring over the fax machines, looking for listing services, sending out RFPs and then cutting purchase orders and so forth, all while the aircraft is sitting on the ground in Stockholm. With the e-market, it's a simple matter to find the nearest supplier that has the chute and determine how fast they can wing it to Sweden. Assuming another example, where time is not of the essence, the e-market would rank-order its chute suppliers by price as well as availability.

Looking at this future through the visionary eyes of Duncan Alexander, doing business through Aerospan is a no-brainer. But how long until his vision becomes reality? Alexander believes that full integration will take about five more years. With a well-thought-out and long-range vision, you get the feeling that Aerospan not only has the right formula, but the strategy and the capability to see it through. Not that Aerospan is alone. It may have been early to the aviation e-marketplace, but several formidable competitors have joined it. On the OEM side, Exostar is testing its wings. On the buyer side, there's Aeroxchange. And as for neutral markets, try Partsbase, Avolo, ILSmart, and Trade Air, to name just a few. Already, however, consolidation is underway. Two players—AirNewco and MyAircraft—have recently merged to form Cordiem.

But Aerospan is no stranger to change. Already, the market's ownership has changed in its short life and it is hardly about to become static. The market will be part of whatever change happens, Alexander foresees. He did not rule out joint ventures, alliances, or even mergers, because his focus is on solutions, not organizational stasis. What gives Aerospan the competitive strength? Consider the following strengths: It can readily tap into the airline buyer community through its parent company, SITA. SITA has developed strong relationships over the past 50 years with its airline members through its private telecommunications network, offering global connectivity to over 700 members. Second, its applications are customized to serve the needs of the air transport community, and it has unique features such as traceability documentation, that critical part-history information so vital in the parts aftermarket. Third, its business-development team continuously works with customers to get feedback and improve marketplace functionality. Finally, it offers an end-to-end procurement solution, from part searches to online purchase orders, and multiple transaction capabilities—bids, direct buying, RFQs, negotiations, and forward and reverse auctions.

And then there are Aerospan's people. Alexander looks for industry skills, but he also believes that e-businesses should hire salespeople who actually have professional selling skills and experience. He also believes that the sales and marketing effort should take place before the business is fully launched. This will get the business past the hype or honeymoon period and into the reality of doing business.

■ FROM TAKEOFF TO MACH 1

Aerospan is clearly in business for the long haul. Its vision—and business plan—calls for flexibility and increasing capabilities over the next few years. Alexander has learned a lesson from the once high-flying start-ups, and he emphasizes the need for solid management skills from the beginning.

Even those B2Bs that have a limited number of customers should be concerned about account management. "Monitor usage," he said. "Do customer follow-ups. Track customer satisfaction. Service the clients you have. Reach out to those who have used the platform or transacted business. Maybe they've used the system and now their usage has slowed down. If so, find out why." Overall, he recommends, it is critical to be curious about what is working well for customers and what problems they may have experienced.

Another of Alexander's secrets is to get heavy-hitters on board. Decision makers probably have no reason to go to your site unless this is already the way they are doing business—and probably it's not yet at this point—so reach out to them and make them believers.

No one ever said that changing the way an industry does business would be easy. Chrisman believes that the biggest challenge ahead for Aerospan is to change the way indi-

viduals within both airlines and their suppliers do business. "We can give them a tool but you can't force them to
use it. We've got proposals out to people to do diagnostics
that show them the benefits and show them how to change
their processes, how to put in place a migration plan to
move their activities online," he says. "That's important
because a lot of people look at this market and they get
overwhelmed by having to change things from the way they
are doing them today."

Clearly, adoption has been slow. Alexander's plan is dis-
armingly simple: "We'll look at the spend, project a certain
percentage of market capture, and then look at the burn
rate to figure out whether the income is sufficient to support the organization. We'll be conservative. We'll be
patient. And have lots of cash."

■ QUESTIONS

Who are the key players in your supply chain that
would need to be included in your exchange to ensure
industrywide adoption?

What big selling point would almost certainly secure
their participation?

What unanticipated challenges did Aerospan run into
that could also occur in your industry and affect your
planning in creating or participating in an exchange?

Part IV

Participating in Net Markets

The money flowed like champagne into dot-com ventures everywhere; and, as everyone knows, free-flowing champagne can lead to one hell of a hangover.

Hackneyed phrase or not, much of the business world has indeed awakened with one hell of a collective, head-splitting hangover. To be fair, the lure of high-flying profits was seductive enough to ensnare even the most ardent tee-totaler.

Eventually, however, the party ends. Like lemmings that run off cliffs, it seems that humans—even executives—can succumb to mass fits of illogic. But the day after brings a startlingly fresh, if not slightly painful, return to logic.

This return to reality brings us back to one of the major themes that we've discussed throughout this book: The fundamentals of business are, in fact, fundamental. *They do not change.* An "e" can be added to the front of every business activity imaginable, but without a solid business plan, a strong customer base, and a sustainable competitive edge, all of the e's in the world mean nothing. Putting false hope into the power of "e" is what caused the hangover in the first place.

For further proof of the immutability of the basics, consider the global research conducted by our A.T. Kearney colleagues James McGrath and Fritz Kroeger to determine the drivers behind sustainable corporate growth. We looked at 1,100 global companies from 1987 to 1998 to find out exactly what it was that enabled some companies to successfully sustain top-line growth for a long period of time, while other companies failed to keep the growth engine alive for any significant length of time at all. Our findings challenge traditional thinking about the way top-line growth should be viewed and understood, and these findings are gathered in *The Value Growers* (2001). For example, we discovered that conscious pursuit of sustainable growth has helped a select group of companies create levels of shareholder value above and beyond what conventional, complacent, or bottom-line-oriented companies generate—and far beyond the returns of companies that grow merely for growth's sake. The five fundamentals of sustainable growth we pinpointed are:

1. Strong, successful growth is possible in any industry, in any region, and at any phase of a business cycle.

2. Strong, stable growth is the decisive drive behind share prices.

3. Innovation, geographic expansion, and risk-taking fuel sustainable growth.

4. Growth is spiral-shaped, rather than linear, which means that every company experiences downturns in the cycle. But top performers use this time to realign resources, establish a better understanding of market dynamics, and redefine their strategies in preparation for the next wave of growth. They invest and turn back to growth.

5. Sustainable growth follows a specific pattern and can be learned.

"Ah," you say. "That study was with old-economy companies. What about Nasdaq firms?" In 2000, A.T. Kearney applied the same measures used in the earlier study to high-tech companies in the new economy. We discovered that what it takes to be a value grower in the old economy is essentially the same in the new economy. The old rules still apply, with one key difference: As a group, value growers in the new economy prefer internal growth over external growth (mergers and acquisitions). So once again, success goes to those that stick with the basics. Whether in the new economy or the old, that is one business rule that does not change.

Ice hockey Power Player Mario Lemieux had an incredible career in the 1990s, and pundits claim that his all-star records would have been even greater if he hadn't had to tussle with a double whammy of Hodgkin's disease and back surgery. The sports legend retired from active playing a few years ago, then purchased the Pittsburgh Penguins and looked for a way to infuse new excitement (and increase ticket sales) in a ho-hum franchise. What star-power could he attract? And then he realized: He was looking at the ultimate draw in the mirror.

Super Mario did not disappoint. He returned to the ice as a player on the team he now owns and showed lesser mortals how the game of hockey should be played. This former Power Player proved that, despite health issues that would have downed a weaker competitor, he could still score goal upon goal and gain the competitive edge.

Lemieux's story serves as metaphor for new-economy business acumen. In the new business arena, your company's role will morph, amoeba-like, among competitor and alliance partner and customer, and it will have to be equally world-class in each role.

In the next few chapters, we turn to the specifics that your company needs to know to be ready for the matrixed world of net markets. Specifically, we are going to examine what you need to know and to think about when you decide to participate in net markets. Because, as Super Mario and corporate Power Players have learned, the fundamentals of doing business in the new economy haven't changed, but some of the details have. And the devil is in the details. In the case of the new economy, the devil brought along plenty of his minions to tempt us away from what we know and trust in business.

What we hope you bring away from this section is a healthy respect for what you already know. Experience and gut instinct, as well as those old notes from Business 101, have a definite place in the world of net markets. But we also encourage you to gain a sense of adventure: Keep your eyes open to the latest developments and their implications for the future. True success nowadays requires a keen eye and a broad perspective as well as a very sensitive gut.

The topics of this section—enterprise transformation, alliances, technology, future-watching—are all perennial favorites, but as you'll read, the new economy offers plenty of twists.

The Challenge of Change Hasn't Changed

A generation of approaches to transforming business enterprises may have kept many management consultants in business, but too frequently the results have not translated into long-term corporate success. It's easy to agree that the development of e-business solutions is demanding an even more dramatic need for change to take full advantage of the opportunities. But genuine transformation—the dynamic and multidimensional challenges of changing the organization to create sustainable performance improvements and of really jumping to the next productivity curve—is easier contemplated than done.

Why did the first round of e-business go to the dot coms, and why did they then turn around and fail so spectacularly? A large part of the reason is that these small organizations had the agility to take advantage of the opportunities, and internal bureaucratic issues were nonexistent, but they didn't have the organizational infrastructure—the time-honored, tried-and-true processes of good management—to maintain their newly competitive positions. That doesn't mean that today's giant enterprises will be able to survive and thrive in the new economy without reorganizing themselves. Indeed, the true value of "e" will never be achieved unless and until these corporations reform themselves internally to take advantage of the opportunities.

We're not talking about creating an Office of the Vice President of E, or of moving the head of the Department of Web-Site Development upstairs to directly report to the CEO. Many of today's blue-chip organizations were never designed to compete in the Internet world, and their post-Industrial Revolution organization chart is as dated as it is pyramidal. Too frequently, key resources are still split across organizational boundaries, decisions are made at the wrong level or too slowly, lessons learned are not disseminated throughout the organization—and worse, each of these bad characteristics is hardwired into the organizational blueprint through the financial reporting structure and process.

Only new structures and new job descriptions with newly conceived responsibilities can change these behaviors and lay the foundation for sustainable success, but this task sometimes seems like reconfiguring a train into an airplane while it is moving: There will be a period in which it will make much more sense to stay a train—and lift-off will be unattractive.

Even in the old economy, it was clear that achieving improved performance demands transformation beyond one-time forays into reengineering, or some other buzzword du jour. To be effective, transformation must confront the single biggest impediment to change—the behavior of people and their beliefs. It must be anchored across the economic, behavioral, and managerial foundations of the organization.

After she tumbled down the rabbit hole, Alice discovered a world "through the looking glass," where everyone was running at full speed—and just managing to stay in place. Like Alice and the Queen, today's senior executives often are confronted with a pace and direction of change that can be erratic and wrenching. No company can hope to survive unless it changes at least as fast as its environment, and like Alice, it must run twice as fast if it hopes to achieve competitive advantage.

Dee Hock, founder and CEO of Visa International, says that "change is not about understanding new things or having new ideas, it's about seeing old things with new eyes—from different perspectives. It's not about reorganizing, reengineering, reinventing, recapitalizing. It's about reconceiving."

In an e-enabled company, all functions and processes are reconceived to take best advantage of the emerging technologies. The changes affect everything the employees touch, and they also do the following:

➤ *Reinforce the corporate culture.* Branding permeates both the organizational intranet and Internet, as well as all interactive communications.

➤ *Personalize interface and information.* Today's all-too-frequent information overload will be managed with personalized pulls and notification of relevant information.

➤ *Create learning communities.* Innovation is facilitated by electronically bringing together physically dispersed experts to develop and share learnings.

➤ *Link corporate databases.* Information about customers, industries, competitors, and organizational know-how is firmwide and easily accessible.

➤ *Provide access to external information.* Already, the corporate library has become increasingly online. It is accessible to all, providing direct links to research providers, leading thinkers, public affairs, and government and legal documents.

➤ *Facilitate knowledge sharing.* Internal best practices are captured and shared across the organization.

➤ *Streamline business processes.* Account information is available online for internal teams and external clients to track and speed activities, facilitate document distribution, and obtain approvals.

➤ *Support employee self-service.* Employees directly update online directories, HR and compensation information, and career development plans.

➤ *Reduce manual administrative tasks.* Employees accomplish time and expense reports online and will link to travel services and billing.

Intuitively, all these attributes sound sensible and desirable. But when preparing a cost-benefit analysis for an auto manufacturer for whom 0.05 percent is a gargantuan savings or for a food retailer for whom 0.05 percent of sourcing cost savings could justify a merger of giants, it is often difficult to quantify the benefits associated with these initiatives in a concrete enough way to justify their costs.

■ MOVING BEYOND FAILURE

The price of survival, now more than ever, is sustainable change—and sustainable change is arduous. Size and uneven global reach do not make matters easier—in fact, just the opposite. Nonetheless, the poor record of virtually *all* transformational models over the past 20 years is hard to rationalize.

The failure rate of various business-process reengineering projects is commonly placed between 50 and 70 percent. Research shows that just one-third of total-quality-management programs in the United States, and one-fifth in the United Kingdom, actually improved competitiveness or showed demonstrable results. Just over one-third of joint ventures survive longer than five years, and according to A.T. Kearney research, more than half of mergers fail to create value.

The conclusion is inescapable: The attempts of most organizations to deliver on the promise of major change efforts have more often than not resulted in embarrassingly high investments and little long-term impact. Furthermore, the advent of the new economy suggests that successful change will become even more elusive, for two important reasons:

➤ *The increasing speed of change.* It is axiomatic to point out that business conditions are changing so rapidly that the old model of corporate behavior—long periods of stability punctuated by periodic adaptation—is no longer viable. By the time one set of changes has been absorbed, the solution is out of date. Because there is no final destination, the goal of change itself has altered dramatically. The aim is no longer the one right solution—the definitive fit between the firm's strategy, structure and systems, and its environment. Instead, the goal is one of *agility*—the ability of the organization to adapt itself almost immediately to changes in its business environment, defined both by its external characteristics and by enabling technologies that can modify the competitive response. In fact, the rate at which an organization learns and changes may be the only form of competitive advantage that is sustainable in the long term.

➤ *The increasing importance of human capital.* When change programs are analyzed to determine the reasons for failure, time and time again the root cause is an insufficient focus on the human factors involved. Seventy percent of *Forbes* 500 CEOs report that the number one block to organizational change is employee resistance, apathy, or unawareness. An A.T. Kearney survey identified cultural mismatches and failure to communicate effectively as two major causes of postmerger problems. Human factors will be even more critical in the future because of the enabling quality of human effort in response to unpredictable situations. Recall Colin Dyer's comments about what he looks for in employees for the WorldWide Retail Exchange: knowledgeable, flexible, and adaptable. Transformation requires knowledge workers who want to, who are able to, and who know how to contribute to change. Command-and-control organizations—and traditional systems in which change is directed from the top—do not fully utilize this pool of human capital.

Defining new goals and aligning people around them requires a recognition that organizations are made up of many different individuals, social groups and networks that flourish across formal structural and hierarchical boundaries. Altering any element of the system affects all the others, making it almost impossible to predict what the result of any particular intervention might be. If you read this last sentence and found yourself agreeing with it, then the discussion on business ecosystems has hit home. Welcome to tomorrow.

■ CHANGING HOW ORGANIZATIONS CHANGE

If we don't learn from our history, we are famously forced to repeat it. Because the odds are that when you read these words—assuming you have been employed in a public firm over the past two years—you will have lived through one major corporate change program, it should be possible for the new economy to learn from the experiences of the old.

Sadly, there is a familiar pattern to most corporate change programs: A clarion call from the CEO is answered with off-site organizational retreats that result in plans and programs with catchy titles. Reorganization, restructuring, and, inevitably, layoffs lead to a plethora of new organization charts. In the end, after all the trauma and dislocation, the results may be a world away from the optimistic targets defined at the outset. In many instances, organizational dynamics—and the processes required to change a multi-billion-dollar institution—are completely underestimated. This usually is not a failure of organizational leadership, but rather a conflict between leadership and management: the result of trying to create an unknowable future while keeping the organization running on target and its stake-holders satisfied with ongoing financial and other goals.

To be effective, genuine transformation must start with an honest appreciation of the complexity of the task. Organizations are constrained by economic, institutional, social, and political dimensions, all of which are defined by the history of the organization and the individuals who work there. That's why what works in one organization may produce disaster in another. To transform itself, the organization needs to understand the nature of both its strengths and limitations.

The art of change involves using the organization's own power and momentum to overcome resistance and to change itself. As a master of aikido uses an opponent's own weight to his advantage, so a change agent must leverage the strengths of the organization to work *with* the change program rather than *against* it. Outflanking the opposition is usually just as important as having the right plan and fielding the right team, and both falter unless the tactics of implementation are executed with precision and finesse.

One string—if pulled with patience and ingenuity—can unravel a complex knot. Similarly, when managed properly, one change action can unblock opportunities throughout the company. Because it is impossible to change one aspect of a company's function without affecting others, full understanding of these interconnections is necessary to take advantage of opportunities to cascade change throughout the organization.

■ ORGANIZATION À LA M.C. ESCHER

One step toward understanding these interactions is to look at the organization from different perspectives—economic, institutional, social, political, and individual. In the same way that a beam of light is both a wave and a stream of particles, depending on the experiment being conducted, so each perspective is more or less true, depending on the point of view of the participant, and recognizing that the observer's perception may change the nature of the organization, too. Together, these perspectives allow the complexity of the organization to be expressed in a manageable way.

➤ It's All about $$$

The most common way of describing an organization is as an economic system that uses labor and capital to add value and reward stakeholders. Parts and labor, balance sheets, and shareholder value form the vocabulary of this economic system. Most e-strategies, up until now, have given this organizational perspective the most attention, which is bizarre; it treats desks as assets and human beings as expenses, and most start-ups don't have a lot of desks, and nowadays human capital is just about the only capital they still have around. A revisit to your old accounting textbook might be in order—FASB concepts are seriously flawed in the new environment.

And that's critical—for start-ups and incumbent firms alike, developing a supporting economic system is obviously critical. Indeed, it was those e-firms that became IPOs without the necessary commerce, content, or connectivity to sustain themselves that had quickly gone to the e-business underworld. However, it's also critical to realize that the economics of the business are changing. After all, as we discussed in Chapter 3, in the e-enabled value chain, the flow of information, the flow of goods, and the flow of economic value each move independently. The split creates at least two separate value chains, in which relative power can be increased independently through consolidation or vertical integration (disintegration).

For example, the fact that FedEx charges $12.00 to deliver a package (the flow of economic value) is unrelated to the movement of that package (the flows of goods) or the effectiveness of the communication contained in the package (the flow of information). In the new economy, the event of Dial charging Delhaize in Durham a certain price for product delivered over a period of time in response to a series of collaboratively developed forecasts of consumer demand will be similarly disaggregated. The model has many successful precedents—we are just not yet comfortable working with them in our more familiar work-a-day environments.

Economic performance is a by-product of other, noneconomic goals—such as satisfying the customer and creating innovative products—all of which are driven or impacted by employee behavior. Understanding how to encourage employees to behave in such a way as to increase economic performance is the secret of initiating and sustaining meaningful change.

➤ In Our Companies We Trust

To implement economic decisions, companies create institutions: rules, roles, and structures that define how employees perform their work. Functions such as human resources and finance, entities such as trade unions and committees, and structures such as job grades and ownership rules are all part of the institutional framework. In the e-economy, it is the institutional perspective that is most dramatically affected.

If misaligned with the needs of business in the new economy, institutional rules can be formidable barriers. Alternatively, innovative changes to institutional systems can create quick wins and demonstrate commitment to becoming an e-organization: intranet-based HR services and time-and-expense reporting, employee-enabled just-in-time training, and corporate messaging are good, quickly implementable examples.

One critical area of alignment in the new economy is reward and performance-measurement systems, which are almost by definition a holdover from previous corporate institutions, and which can be a major hindrance if they either measure the wrong things or, in their simplicity, stifle rather than foster creativity and motivation. For example, some old-line companies actually constrained employees' personal use of the company's Internet access for the same reasons they constrained personal use of the company's telephones, until they realized that moderate and appropriate use of the Net actually increases employee productivity. Reward and performance-management systems that measure the success of a point solution rather than the success of multifunctional processes reflect old-economy thinking. Consider these examples: for the vertically integrated own-label apparel retailer, least first cost rather than sell-through at list price; for the manufacturer of industrial equipment, cost per piece per purchase order rather than fully adjusted gross margin per unit; for the law firm, utilization rather than profitability per professional.

Now, these new measures make most corporate accounting departments wriggle with anxiety. But the new technology not only sends coupons for movie discounts to your telephone, it also provides a much more powerful mechanism for capturing, linking, and aggregating information than ever before. Old-school ABC (activity-based costing) pales in comparison with the potential for powerful and revealing analytic reward and performance tools. But these tools are just that: tools. Human beings still have to figure out what it is that makes their businesses successful, and, therefore, what they want to measure.

Sometimes, established companies will attempt to foster a new way of thinking by physically distancing the exploratory pod from the mother ship. The temptation to control innovation nearly to death is very strong, however, and some otherwise successful companies just can't let their children grow up without enculturation in the traditional way of thinking. When IBM set up its PC division in the early 1980s, it deliberately excluded the new unit—institutionally and geographically—from the larger institutional structure in order to encourage breakthrough thinking. Under the leadership of Don Estridge, a skunk works "down in Boca [Raton]" was given carte blanche to ignore the bureaucracy and hierarchy in IBM's Armonk, New York, headquarters.

Unfortunately, when the division outgrew its incubator, IBM brought the renegade back into the fold. This served to suppress institutional structures, which, if they had been allowed to grow and challenge the status quo, might have saved Big Blue much subsequent trouble. Similarly, GM tried to let Saturn create its own free-range car division, but while some innovations still remain, others—like new product design and development—appear to have fallen into traditional patterns. Ford's idea of moving Lincoln-Mercury marketing out of Detroit and three time zones away to California is meeting with a bit more success. "With Ford and Mercury both headquartered in Detroit, you had designers and engineers working on Taurus four days a week, Sable one day a week. Now that Mercury is separate, we can work on Sable five days a week and come up with a different car," says Jim Rogers, Lincoln-Mercury's award-winning marketing honcho.

➤ Can We Talk?

Organizations are as much social entities as they are economic and institutional ones. Despite economic and institutional rhetoric—shareholder value, customer value, and corporate mission—employees are socially motivated. The reality is that people come to work to earn money, but they also come to interact with others in a social setting, and they succeed when they are part of something that helps define their identity.

About 10 years ago, the business press was filled with articles about how people-friendly organizations were rewarding valued employees with telecommuting options. Meanwhile, management cognoscenti were anticipating a time in the not-too-distant future when corporations would insist that their employees work from home or get involved in a hoteling arrangement in order to save on expensive real estate, typically the second largest expense to the corporate bottom line. But to date, this 1990s prediction of an officeless company has proved as accurate as 1970s forecasts about the paperless office.

Why? The predictors failed to comprehend the social environment in which most people prefer to work. People are more likely to share workplace gossip (and serious information) in the hallways than via more formal methods. Moreover, teamwork—the real backbone of the new economy—can be facilitated with electronic communication media, but only after face-to-face, real-time discussions confirm the humans' ability to interact via more sophisticated technologies.

Organizations can't afford to ignore this social dimension. Not only do people seem to prefer to work in proximity to one another, but ever since Western Electric's groundbreaking Hawthorne experiments of the 1920s and 1930s that showed the productivity-enhancing power of collaborative change itself was more telling than the content of the change, it has been clear that the organization's social system exerts a powerful influence on productivity, behavior, and creativity of employees.

Social pressure may increase productivity, but it also can affect change, invisibly but powerfully. The referential power of leaders—the power to model desired behavior through their own actions—is at least as effective as the formal power their positions represent. A leader who visibly walks the talk will be more effective in promoting change than one who does not. Similarly, hierarchical companies can find it hard to kick-start project teams that bring junior and senior staff together in uncomfortable proximity.

Global diversity adds yet more complexity, and approaches that work well in the United States may have quite different results in Europe or Asia. Take, for example, a global retailer like Ahold. At first blush you would think of Ahold as a preeminent Dutch retailer. In addition, of course, Ahold is an important food retailer and food-service provider in the United States. But in fact, Ahold operates in 25 countries, and has over 8,500 stores outside these two markets. It is these stores, this business, that can benefit the most from the playing-field-leveling, technology-enabling characteristic of e-commerce. If Ahold needs e-business anywhere, it's not in the Netherlands, it's in Phuket, Thailand. If you think your company is immune to this almost amazing degree of globalization, think of those ball bearings that were sourced from Hungary, or the green beans from Argentina. Not your examples? If you don't have similar examples in your company, then you should probably be reading up on the benefits that can be achieved from more effective sourcing!

Perhaps the most powerful example of a global e-business is i2's Aspect software business, which works to accumulate and disseminate billions, and probably soon trillions, of data regarding products of all kinds throughout the work-through web-enabled networks hooked up with software tools in front of and behind your firewall—and this engine is powered by thousands of people working away in Banga-lore, literally on the other side of the Earth from where most of this information is put to best use.

➤ Everyone's Hidden Agenda

Management's great unspoken taboo is organizational pol-itics. Politics, rarely mentioned even in management lit-erature, is presumed not to exist in a healthy organization. "Playing politics" is frequently the worst accusation that can be thrown at an employee. According to convention, office politics is off-limits because it smacks of manipula-tion and hidden agendas.

But let's be honest. Politics is the universal currency of power and influence, and it is grist to the mill of creativity and innovation. In every organization, new economy as well as old, unofficial fixers and influencers, old guards and young power brokers, build shifting coalitions that play a large, and sometimes dominating, role in what gets done and how. The trick should be not to eliminate politics or to pretend it doesn't exist, but to use it to get the job done.

Political power often bears no relation to institutional hierarchy. All good corporate politicos know that the low-ranking assistant who sits in front of the executive's office—and controls the day-to-day flow of paper and information into that office—may be a far more potent friend or foe than is the executive-boss. This is not an idle or foolish example. In this transitional period, in which many very powerful executives still do not view their own e-mail, the politics of the bureaucratic structures that surround them are of extreme sensitivity and importance. Politics looms particularly large in companies with complex matrix structures (because of the multiple power centers and the need to build up the network while still satisfying the requirements of the hierarchy) and in companies undergoing institutional transformations. Reading the organizational charts may be instructive, but these charts frequently bear little or no resemblance to the informal network or the real way decisions are made and implemented.

Perhaps Steve Jobs at Apple is the most newsworthy example of this formal/informal organization style. As founder and godfather, he presaged the transformation not only of Apple, but of the computer industry in general, which was epochal for IBM, and totally devastating for Digital Equipment Corp. John Sculley stripped Jobs of his power and kicked him off the board, and when Jobs, phoenixlike, returned to Apple, it was not as CEO or chief anything, but as ... well, what's the term? Guru? Chief dude? For a while Jobs had no official position, but politically, he was the only guy that counted. If you don't have a Steve Jobs in your company, well, why not?

Executives cannot ignore the political dimension of change. Stepping up communication and striving to create consensus will be ineffective against determined political opponents who will find a million ways to slow down, distract, and derail that change. Political issues are much easier to deal with once they have been uncovered and legitimized, and executives must be prepared to discuss the undiscussable. Political insight, compromise, and negotiation are an integral part of the change toolkit.

➤ What about Me?

Sure, people come to work for the paycheck. But they stay and are motivated by the entire value proposition that the company—consciously or unconsciously—provides for them. This includes their sense of belonging and their needs, aspirations, and desires.

In the old days, there was an enormous temptation to treat people as separate groups, to talk of "the shop floor" or of "middle management." After a lifetime of working in one of these groups, an employee would retire with a dinner and a gold watch, and the satisfaction of a job well done. But that was then.

Many employees are having their world substantially change by the new economy. Traditional jobs and roles are disappearing, and new roles are being created, requiring different and as-yet scarce skills. Traditional escalator careers are being replaced by new and sometimes unpleasant whirling-teacup careers: great experiences, and you're getting around, but, man! shouldn't there be a better way? New-economy organizations need more than key technical skills, they are looking for fit and entrepreneurial savvy to compete in a world where the competitive landscape can be reinvented in a short 90 days.

Knowledge workers are not another quantifiable organizational asset, to be deployed and reconfigured like machine tools. Key workers are requiring more than financial inducements to stay with the organization. Loyalty—or lack thereof—is affected by these workers' personal knowledge that hard work frequently did not keep their parents from getting a pink slip in the 1980s and 1990s. And if you are a senior exec, you may want to read that last sentence one more time—the middle-management go-nowhere you RIFed in 1986? His daughter is running your supply-chain e-business planning department now....

So how does an organization hire and retain the knowledge workers it needs? The new employee contract is more akin to Franklin D. Roosevelt's lend-lease program than to the corporate gold watch. Today, knowledge workers provide their capabilities to the company in exchange for salary and benefits. The employee works hard and, when the term of employment is over, both sides depart satisfied: The company has had the full involvement of a valued employee, and the employee has gained experience and know-how during the period of engagement. Very Taoist, this: nobody ever leaves; they just aren't there anymore—or, put a different way, they aren't adding incremental value anymore. But you are further ahead than when they came, aren't you?

■ POWER TO THE PEOPLE

If people are neither as predictable nor as sequentially rational as traditional change programs presuppose, they are generally sensible and positive in intention. In this light, the term "resistance to change" is misleading. People who resist change usually do so for *good* reasons, mostly because the change conflicts with their personal set of economic, social, or political priorities. Personal interests are neither right nor wrong, but they may be compatible or incompatible with the aims of the change process. Many resisters may be turned into supporters when their reasons are recognized and addressed. For transformational leaders, this, indeed, is perhaps the most critical task: outflanking the opposition.

Armed with these perspectives, the change leader can better understand why people behave the way they do, and how they might be encouraged to behave differently. These insights can be translated into action through plans, targets, interventions, and projects that address change across all aspects of the organization. Although every program will be tailored to the particular history and aspirations of the organization, seven major tasks must be undertaken. An effective program must do these things:

➤ *Create a compelling case for change.* The leadership team must articulate the rationale, goals, and scope of the change process in a way that makes it compelling to the organization's key stakeholders. Tim Koogle, who built Yahoo! and served as its CEO until earlier this year, often said that he changed the way his people thought about what Yahoo! was set to do. Most employees thought they were creating the best web browser, the best search engine, the preeminent Internet community, yada, yada, yada. Tim put it in a way that described the messianic fervor. "It was like a newsroom. Each morning we would come in and read the press releases that had hit the wire that night. And then we would spend the day responding to them." By energizing his people with the real and present rather than the theoretical and somewhere-but-not-here, Koogle, who continues as chairman, has built an extremely tough Internet environment.

➤ *Manage change in an integrated fashion.* A true transformation program can be an immensely complex endeavor, and include many interactions and trade-offs. Program-management procedures, structures, and processes that monitor benefits must be developed to ensure that the program achieves its goals. Team members must be recruited and dedicated to the task in hand under clear and powerful leadership. Rolls-Royce's transformation program, for example, is very ambitious and complex to manage. At the end of 1999, the airplane engine maker pulled together all its e-business strategy programs—which up to that time had been spread among its various business units—and created a single, corporatewide program office. The new director identified three main areas of e-business opportunities within Rolls-Royce—within the supply chain, internal processes, and customer facing—and, armed with this information, was able to prioritize the projects and to productively expand upon the initiatives.

➤ *Align, engage, and mobilize leadership.* The CEO must build a leadership team united around and capable of driving the change. Of course you want to uncover and address differences of opinion and political tensions. Everyone looks to leadership, not for words, but for actions, and in the long run, leadership behavior will largely determine the success of the program. Jack Welch's now-famous division of managers into four groups demonstrates the importance of aligned leadership. His subdivisions? Those who deliver on commitments, those who do not, those who believe in the corporate values, and those who do not. Ultimately, managers who wish to succeed in GE must demonstrate both their commitment and their ability to deliver. Things haven't changed in the e-economy. Make your new four-celled e-matrix of those who get it and those who don't, plus those who make progress against those who don't. Nobody's going to buy three years of bad results just because you're working on the Internet!

➤ *Align, engage, and mobilize stakeholders.* A critical mass of the organization's stakeholders must be committed to the change objectives. It's important to assess current and required social norms and culture. Change leaders should identify key stakeholders and engage them in the program. Then they must communicate goals and results in a meaningful way to employees to enable them to support the transformation, and to believe that the difficult changes are worthwhile. That used to be an expensive and difficult proposition. Back at Rolls-Royce, the leadership brought together 25,000 employees to spend a full day, in groups of 15 to 20 people, to discuss the competitive situation and the need for radical performance improvements. Today, e-mail, intranets, and videoconferences can offer two-way conversations that, if deployed successfully, can provide similar results at a fraction of the investment.

➤ *Align measurement systems.* Performance measures that align with the new ways of working reinforce expected behaviors. Information technology and management systems installed make the measures operational. A global telecommunications company implemented a web-based process for embedding service quality excellence, for example. The program included both an e-enabling tool and improved business processes. As a result, the organization identified benefits of $205 million over a three-year period.

➤ *Implement new processes and technologies.* Economic returns are ultimately delivered through business processes, and, to fit the change program, they likely need to be e-designed. Leadership needs to push new technology systems because the organization will be chary about doing it on their own, and leadership will need to push with clear objectives and a solid idea of the benefits that these systems can deliver, including their role as a coordinated, multidirectional communications system. At one global healthcare products company, the move from strategic sourcing to e-procurement included change management and business training. As a result of the program, the company identified savings of $80 million annually, and it is now rolling out e-procurement to its European business units.

➤ *Build a capable and competent organization—and know the difference between the two.* Change leaders must develop a new organizational model in which the economic, institutional, social, and political systems are aligned with the change goals and with each other. The organization must define and create new competencies and capabilities, and it must install new structures and management systems to sustain the change and drive continuous improvement and organizational fluidity. Creating this change capability can take many forms, and one that is growing in popularity is the concept of the corporate university. Human resources and training initiatives designed to promote "e" options at a global health-care company, paired with development of an enterprise portal, have realized $40 million in total savings and productivity gains, as well as enhanced employee services. Part of the ongoing savings came from self-service human resources options, which cut the cost of individual HR transactions by an average of 30 percent. As HR transaction costs increase throughout the developed world, such impressive productivity gains should not be discounted. Capable means you can do it; competent means you can do it day in and day out.

■ GETTING TO "YES"

Enterprise transformation must have economic, institutional, political, social, and human objectives. There are many trade-offs and constraints to be articulated and embedded in the program design. Which processes and technologies must be deployed? Which specific behaviors of individuals are required, and in what circumstances? Which parts of the business system need to be changed to encourage these behaviors? Which aspects of the institution must change to support the desired behaviors and circumvent possible minefields? What political issues will be raised, and what action needs to be taken to respond to them? Which social networks and norms encourage—and discourage—desired behavior?

Of course, no generalized answers will be available to such questions at the start of the transformation process, so the program must be continuously refined in the light of events that come up as the process moves forward. While the program vision and objectives should remain stable throughout the transition, tactics and plans must continuously evolve. One of our favorite models, an organization that is going through the momentous changes required by transforming their organization to exploit the web: When we counsel such an organization, we offer a one-hour session at 6:00 P.M. every evening over the weeks we are engaged for anyone who is interested. No RSVPs are required, but are the rooms full? You betcha. And do we get results in the buyer organization, the merchant organization, the engineer organization? You probably already know the answer.

A CEO who embarks on the hazardous and unpredictable journey toward change steps into an uncomfortable, taxing, challenging, and very squishy world that can be traversed only if approached with commitment and energy and with a willingness to leave sight of the shore in order to arrive at the destination across the sea. A consensus must be built around the new orthodoxy, often in the face of initial incomprehension, disbelief, and mistrust. The more profound the change, the more effort the CEO will need to devote to understanding behavioral drivers and building the coalitions that will embrace the new thinking. But don't forget about this quarter's earnings! Demand that every four-year program be broken down into 12 three-month programs, each of which has a sensible and believable return on investment. If you're a $10 billion enterprise, and some consultant has promised a $400 million benefit, then you should target at least $20 million of benefit from any individual undertaking.

The leadership team should think twice about implementing plans that they would not be willing to discuss openly, and they must maintain respect for colleagues who oppose—or remain neutral toward—the transformation. They must also set high expectations and consistently exhibit the behaviors they wish others to adopt—with all the scrutiny that this implies.

Enterprise transformation nearly always requires executives to change as much as, or more than, rank-and-file employees. Improving organizational capability requires leaders to *surrender* direct control, to stop managing and begin to really lead. Mobilizing an organization's political energy rather than ignoring or fighting it will build the momentum to keep the organization moving forward.

Although change can be a daunting prospect, change leaders must, in the final analysis, ask themselves if they really have a choice: Will the business environment become more or less stable? Will "e" have more or less impact than it does today? Will competition increase or decrease? Are the old ideas of hierarchical control, periodic restructurings, and silver bullets really sustainable in the new economy? Transformation is complex, unpredictable, and uncomfortable. It is, however, *the* leadership competence of the future.

■ QUESTIONS

How do you transform an organization into a learning organization? This concept has been around for a long time, but it is especially important now. How can you bring the right new people into the organization at the same time that you are retraining deeply functional people in the new process orientation required to win in the new environment?

How do you assess the agility of your organization? Where would you put your skunk works? Can you identify the individual people in your organizational that you would tap in order to make it happen in your company? How would you keep from restricting their creativity?

With the increasing speed of change, how do you encourage your employees to be loyal to the organization? Is your company fun, fast, and forward? Or do you need to get it there? Or not? Do you succeed with a different business model?

Chapter 11

The Competitor Dating Game

In the old century, many of the Power Players tried to forge real alliances with value-chain partners—it was seen as competitive advantage and an opportunity. Despite their best intentions, most alliances failed to produce the intended results. In the current century, forging alliances has become a required core competency for the Power Players—and the partners with whom alliances must be formed include competitors.

For years, companies have sung the praises of partnerships without ever really getting serious about forming them. In hindsight, it is easy to see that few companies understood the vigorous commitment that forging a true partnership would require. Or if they did know, they sure didn't let on about it. Okay, buyers and suppliers mastered the jargon necessary to communicate their alliances: "We are one team. We're strategically aligned. We share a common vision." But few companies ever really got their arms around what it meant to be full-fledged partners—a failure later manifested in the fact that most long-standing alliances produce too few tangible results.

Suddenly, what was once considered nice but not necessary is recognized as very necessary, but that doesn't make forging partnerships any easier. In theory, the strategy is simple. Bring together a network of companies that share a value chain to establish or exploit an e-marketplace, and structure the network in such a way that all members are able to share the information necessary to create an alliance infrastructure—and then assess the value each brings to the endeavor to better apportion among the partners the benefits that have been created. "Piece of cake" comes to mind, no?

■ WHEN GOLIATHS GET TOGETHER

Did anyone really think the corporate Goliaths would sit back and allow the many Davids—such as your typical dot-com companies—to step between them and their suppliers or customers? No, of course not. But then again, no one really thought the many Goliaths would get together and devise a solution that would require building a coalition of competitors. The more likely scenario had companies forging proprietary exchanges like Wal-Mart's, in which companies built a network of their own suppliers and supply-chain groupies and their competitors would do the same.

Proprietary exchanges are hard to argue with because they have been overwhelmingly successful. The focus is on one-to-one transactions and leveraging the technology backbone and infrastructure that is the offshoot of having multiple one-to-one relationships. For example, Cisco has parlayed its thousands of suppliers into a network, as has Wal-Mart and GM and countless other companies. Indeed, Wal-Mart revolutionized the retail industry by using existing information-management techniques and logistics systems to separate the flow of information from the flow of goods. In essence, Wal-Mart created a new value proposition—and in doing so, it has worked its way into the number-one retailing position. Now with a major technology upgrade for its private RetailLink e-hub, Wal-Mart has opted to run its own private marketplace rather than join a public exchange—for now, at least. In truth, the real honor to Wal-Mart comes from its willingness to try—again and again—to get it right. The company is surprisingly daring and innovative—and knows when to hold, fold, or run.

Cisco's networked supply chain is just as busy. Globally, more than 90 percent of Cisco product orders are placed via the Internet, and that figure is closer to 100 percent in Europe. Cisco's supply partners fulfill more than half of these orders with no assistance or involvement from Cisco employees.

So, if private exchanges work so well, why aren't more companies building them? In most cases, the answer lies in an age-old problem: money. Building a private exchange is an expensive proposition. Most of the corporations that initiate private exchanges are well funded and can foot the bill of establishing connections to their trading partners. The only other way to go is to build an independent exchange, but this route tends not to have the same funding capabilities, forcing companies to raise funds in the private or public market—and given where the public market is headed, these exchanges face some true challenges in the short term.

By early 2000, industry-based public exchanges were fast becoming an alternative to the expensive proposition of building either a private exchange or an independent exchange—and this changes the value proposition for proprietary exchanges: Remember our earlier comment about Chemdex and changing business models?

■ BIG, BIGGER, BIGGEST

At first glance, the benefit of partnering with competitors is a no-brainer. The WWRE's 53 members boast that they have combined market power in the form of joint sales approaching $800 billion, or about three and a half times that of Wal-Mart's. Sears, as a founding member of Global-NetXchange (GNX) was talking about moving between $5 and $7 billion in annual spending to the exchange, representing about 75 percent of its procurement. Now, Royal Dutch Ahold says 50 percent of its purchases will run through the WWRE by 2010.

With numbers like these, and the cost/benefit analyses, attracting members can be a snap. It helps, too, that the whole theory behind alliance building is well established. After all, most of the entrepreneurial start-ups on the Internet made their ambitious plans achievable by creating alliances with carefully selected partners. Yahoo!, for one, knew that being born on the Internet was not enough to ensure true worldwide penetration. In a move that was considered extremely risky at the time, former CEO Tim Koogle ignored textbook thinking and decided to expand into markets outside North America, despite the risk of spreading the company too thin. His reasoning? The potential rewards were too compelling to pass up. Yahoo! also realized it lacked internal resources to build the type of content that it needed to fulfill its vision of being an "info-mediary," so it set up content-sharing partnerships with content powerhouses Ziff-Davis (the New York–based high-technology publishing firm) and Reuters. Koogle had no intention of competing head-to-head with monster providers of original content.

Consider, also, the recent strategic partnering of i2 Technologies and A.T. Kearney. The alliance offers the first integrated solution to help companies complete a full e-sourcing and e-procurement transformation. In addition to automating the requisitioning process, the alliance helps companies embed state-of-the-art strategic sourcing methods into the organization and set up private net markets. The result is that companies will realize and sustain true savings by eliminating maverick spending, rationalizing the supply base, improving contract compliance, creating more cost effective product designs, and creating category-specific supply-chain solutions.

Alliances have also been at the heart of traditional companies moving onto the Internet. Case in point: DoveBid Inc. Started in 1937 as Dove Brothers LLC, a San Francisco–based B2B capital-assets auction and valuation-services company, it enjoyed great success being rooted in the old economy. Ross Dove, grandson of the founder and current CEO and chairman, easily could have continued going with the flow. After all, business was good. But after watching a stock report on television that showcased the rapid rise of eBay, the groundbreaking C2C auction site, Dove couldn't shake the notion that some smart person should create a similar platform for the business of liquidating assets. Eventually, he did.

In November 1999, DoveBid Inc. was launched. The site offers both Webcast and online capital asset auctions, as well as an array of value-added B2B services. Alliances and partnerships formed the bedrock behind DoveBid's growth and success. Partnerships include: AssetsB2B, a Hong Kong-based auctioneer of used and idle assets for Asia-Pacific and North American markets; semiconbay.com, a provider of B2B, auction, and exchange services for the semiconductor industry; and BioBid, Inc., a California-based online marketplace for high-end pre-owned biotechnology and pharmaceutical capital assets.

In addition, DoveBid has expanded its reach through relationships with companies involved in MRO material management services (Cameron & Barkley), MRO procurement (iProcure), asset maintenance management (Datastream), and asset inventory services (Seguer International Inc.). DoveBid also is a charter sponsor of the Yahoo! B2B Marketplace (b2b.yahoo.com).

■ WHAT'S IN IT FOR ME?

Granted, industry players have the motivation and compelling reasons to partner, but can die-hard competitors really cooperate? Really?

"The easy part has been our ability to come together," explains Edith Kelly-Green, interim CEO at Aeroxchange, the coalition e-marketplace serving the airline industry. "When you have 13 different airlines trying to put together a company, you would expect that it would be difficult," she said. "But relative to other organizations that come together with that number of participants, it's been much easier than I expected. We had a common need, so the process of getting there was simpler."

In a coalition, it is not so much what will benefit one company but what will benefit all companies. This poses the more complicated question, and one that only the relevant exchange and not the participating members can answer, "What services should be provided to make the exchange attractive for *all* members?" While the answer to this question will change as e-marketplaces evolve, one word continues to crop up over and over again: *Value.* Alliances will form between competitors and noncompetitors alike for one reason only—to create value.

"The industry players have the burning desire—between them and all their trading partners—to improve and attack the inefficiencies, and they understand them better than anybody," said Rick Herbst, chief strategy officer for Transora.

In A.T. Kearney's own 2001 study of the high-tech industry, we found that coalition members want nothing more than to strengthen already well-established relationships with their strategic partners. The same song was being sung in many industries, from consumer products to aerospace and high-tech. Companies are happy with their given set of partners and simply want to use the Internet and the new technology to make improvements.

To attract members, industry-based exchanges began by offering basic e-procurement functions such as order processing, payment processing, and order delivery, as well as the auction and the reverse auction. Soon after, the exchanges moved on to the more ambitious goal of managing supply-chain functionality, and offering services in

CPFR. Findings in the recent A.T. Kearney strategy study confirmed these results. We found that if an industry-based exchange focuses solely on procurement or procurement-related services, it, and its members, would never get to liquidity.

■ GREATER THAN THE SUM OF ITS PARTS

The implications of improving supply-chain functions are impressive. In an exchange, suppliers are able to avoid a hefty cost in stored inventory by letting their larger customers place and track orders online, as they need them. Already, Sears reports that its participation in GNX is responsible for reducing its safety stock while continuing to ensure that it has the right products at the right time—simply by sharing real-time online demand data with manufacturer partners.

"If retailers and manufacturers can bring down inventory levels even a fraction, it will be a huge cost savings," said Joe Laughlin, a former Sears executive who is now chief executive officer of GNX. Once Sears and its suppliers set targets to bring down inventories, they should also be able to optimize production schedules as a result of sharing real-time demand and actual production capacity.

Industry-based e-marketplaces are breathing new life into the concept of efficient replenishment. The concept dates back more than a decade in the grocery industry to when trading partners cut costs, streamlined distribution, and improved customer service using efficient consumer response (ECR). The rewards were substantial. Grocery distributors' gross margins rose more than 2 percent, and partners saw their inventories (on average) decline by more than 20 percent. Now, every e-marketplace in every industry is shaking off the cobwebs of ECR theory.

Logistics is a compelling reason to join an e-marketplace. Converge (formerly eHITEX), a coalition of companies headed by Hewlett-Packard (HP) and E2open (the competing IBM-led coalition), has made a concerted effort to go beyond procurement offerings to strike alliances with various logistics providers. Now, Converge says that the time it takes to arrange, manage, track, and monitor shipments in transit has gone from days and hours to minutes. Freight carriers, shippers, and third-party logistics providers can accurately track, and monitor members' transportation assets—and the cargo they contain—from origin to destination throughout the world. In fact, web-native software companies such as Arzoon have achieved significant revenue traction, solving the logistics problem.

Offering online alliances with financial services providers is another way to attract potential members to an e-marketplace. In fact, in the A.T. Kearney study, participants said that if they hadn't seen these types of additional services they would never have joined the exchange in the first place.

Information flow is key to attracting manufacturers. We know that speed is of the essence in scheduling capacity use, but schedulers typically don't get adequate information fast enough to make schedule changes when new demand arises. In an e-marketplace, the right information theoretically gets to the right people quickly, enabling the manufacturer to fill up momentary bits of capacity. By improving asset management, the manufacturer can get more productivity out of existing plants and thus reduce the need for new manufacturing facilities. And that's just the beginning. Think about how order management takes place via the Internet.

Alliance members are able to eliminate intermediate billing among supply-chain partners and express all payments as a percentage of sales to the consumer. With inventory levels reduced to between 30 and 60 days (except for seasonal items), every member of the exchange improves its cash flow. And, each partner is immediately credited with its share of the sale at the time a consumer buys the product.

Consider the implications for the automotive industry. Rather than an automaker sending an order to its tire supplier, the tire supplier goes to the automaker's online production schedule. The supplier, knowing its percentage of the OEM's business, generates orders to replenish its tires based on the production schedule. The supplier then ships the tires from a warehouse next door, relieving it of its transportation responsibility. Eventually, automakers will be able to pay their tire suppliers after the tires are mounted on the cars, or after the dealer sells the cars. This will be possible using an online tracking system that extends to the dealer, determining first that a car has been sold, and then that it was equipped with tires—for example, with four steel-belted radials.

Many companies join an industry exchange for the collaborative opportunities. Collaboration is necessary in terms of planning, forecasting, or replenishment, which we have already talked about. Collaboration is also relevant to product design and product development. In product design, for example, manufacturers that contract out segments of their design and manufacturing processes to specialists often struggle to communicate specification changes among multiple vendors.

In an e-marketplace, however, companies can respond quickly to shifting requirements from many sources without losing control of the process. In fact, change-control managers can make change approval a daily occurrence— monitoring and approving product alterations online rather than at special meetings or negotiation sessions. For retailers, the benefits are increased time to market for new product introductions, fewer reworks and errors, and better return on assets invested in development efforts.

Collaboration is said to be the highest goal of e-marketplace activity, but this is not the case for all companies. For technology companies, where product design and product development are big sources of competitive advantage, there is an understandable reluctance to share information. This clearly limits the membership benefits for technology companies, which is ironic given that alliances with technology companies are otherwise critical for the success of any e-marketplace.

■ THE ALLIANCE HIT PARADE

Every e-marketplace must forge its share of technology alliances in order to meet its strategic goals. For Covisint to get up and running, for example, it had to build technology alliances with SAP, Commerce One, and Oracle. Similarly, Transora has agreements with i2, IBM, UCCnet, and Ariba, among others. Converge has contracts with SAP, Commerce One, RosettaNet, and Celarix. WWRE and E2open were among the first to select the highly touted e-business alliance of IBM, i2, and Ariba.

Technology alliances tend to be stronger than other types of alliances for one very important reason—they are critical to success. For example, the technology alliances formed by industry-based public exchanges are driven by players that have the capital to lock them in. Covisint's desire to take an equity stake in Commerce One had an obvious impact on that alliance.

Not long ago, the independent e-marketplaces seemed to have a technological leg up on the consortia-based e-marketplaces, but that was before companies such as Ariba, Commerce One, and i2 Technologies developed off-the-shelf programs that could be customized to the needs of individual industries. These new products have changed the nature of technology and are working better than the customized technology of the earlier companies. According to Jupiter Research, 70 percent of the consortia-led e-marketplaces will have an advantage over the early companies in offering services for collaboration and supply-chain project management.

Also, technological connectivity between e-marketplaces and tier-one and tier-two suppliers is being jump-started by partnerships formed between e-marketplaces. For example, to automatically replenish inventory, e-markets are establishing the technological wherewithal to mediate between companies. So the toy inventory of Toys "R" Us, and its purchasing processes and logistics, can be aligned with those of Kenner and Hasbro.

In essence, technology is smoothing the path to true integration. At its recent symposium, members of Transora, the Chicago-based exchange created by 50 major consumer packaged-goods companies, discussed the goals of its "many-to-many technology solution." The concept: Supplier exchanges connect to manufacturer exchanges, which in turn connect to retail exchanges. Transora, in effect, becomes a single point of connectivity.

Consortia e-marketplaces have an ace up their sleeve to back up an already strong hand: the credibility of their founders. Obviously, members are attracted to industry-based alliances because of the inherent industry knowledge and strategic connections. That knowledge doubles and even triples as companies form their own unique alliances. For example, one of Transora's trading affiliates is Novopoint, another e-marketplace and food-and-beverage coalition, whose CEO explains this reasoning most succinctly: "We're taking the domain expertise of the food industry and coupling it with people who have banking experience and logistics experience," says Bob Schult. "When you create something new like this, you have to put people with different backgrounds together to solve this puzzle. One of the critical pieces is the experience with the food business."

Yet getting to the point where companies share inventory, purchase processes, and logistics will take another couple of years, given retailers' relative lack of investment in technology to date and the notoriously dated and inflexible legacy systems that some still have that must be adapted or replaced to accommodate e-markets. We will discuss these issues in Chapter 12.

Clearly, many challenges still remain. In any coalition where there are multiple players, there will be governance issues and politics: How much do I want to participate? How much information do I get? How much information do I give away? At the end of the day, these companies are still competitors and will remain so for years to come. These issues will be resolved if, and only if, *all* of the parties in an e-marketplace prosper.

■ QUESTIONS

Is it better to build a private exchange than to join an industry-based e-net market? How do you assess the value of each: is the relatively higher cost of private exchanges covered by better returns? Are your processes so strategic or your information so confidential that the added cost of a proprietary exchange makes sense? Can you do it faster, better, cheaper? Does an industry-based or public exchange have a business model that makes sense for you? Are your competitors getting together to create an industry-sponsored e-market? Want to have a seat at the table?

What about standards? Are they relevant or important in your industry? Will the exchange be the vehicle through which standards are created and transmitted?

How can you determine which net market is the best for your organization? Aside from the press releases, what is the strategic direction of the exchanges in which you are interested? Do you have a personal conversation going on with the executives in the exchange? Do you have an internal plan in place to implement many of the elements that are being targeted by available exchanges?

What about alliances with other players in your value chain? Are they hooking up with exchanges? Does your industry lend itself to information-based infrastructures for alliances?

Do you have an effective sales and operations planning process, where real sales forecasts get into your production planners before they have to lock down their schedules? (Before you answer this question, you might just want to double-check.)

Chapter 12

Setting the Global Standard for Standards

It is increasingly difficult to stay ahead of the technological curve. Ask any chief technical officer who has set teams of people to research the high-tech market for the most flexible, most advanced business systems only to discover that today's biz has suddenly become yesterday's buzz. Or ask anyone who has considered joining a net market, only to learn that integrating current systems with those that the techno set claim will transport the company back to the future is a nail-biting experience at best.

Yes, the future of business rests on the most up-to-date technology. The Internet and flexible IT systems and net markets all hold the promise of security and seamless, integrated operations. The miracle of the Internet—and of the net markets it supports—is its seemingly infinite capacity for scalability. Anywhere a telephone or a satellite can reach, and where you can put a $1,000 computer, you're there. That's scalable in Sri Lanka, in the suburbs of Cairo, and in the backlands of Xinjiang.

However, technology alone does not permit seamless communication. Seamless communication takes standards—global standards. And we ain't anywhere near there; the current landscape is riddled with competing standards.

How many standards? Forrester Research surveyed 50 online marketplaces and discovered that almost three-quarters are deploying proprietary software. Such systems run contrary to the greater good of the net market, and they will continue to block the level of seamless e-commerce that net markets are capable of delivering.

"It's a chicken-and-egg problem," says Evelyn Cronin, a senior B2B analyst with Gartner Group in the United Kingdom. "It's hard work to get many companies to agree on processes and catalog numbers [and other protocols] for the betterment of the whole industry. But it's harder to get trading partners to go online if there aren't any standards."

So despite the marvels of technology, the real key to success in net markets is in establishing rules: rules to exchange information over the Internet and rules to define universal data standards. Make no mistake. Understanding these two basic requirements will not only give you insight into where net markets are headed, it will also help you decipher the viability of the overwhelming number of technological options you face today.

■ GETTING THE TRAINS TO RUN ON TIME

One of the reasons we talk about standards is to make our computers run on time. Enter the metaphor of the train system: The basic technology of steam or electricity is the motive engine that drives the train. In B2B, the engine can be compared to computer technology: binary code, electromagnetic management of data, silicon-chip technology, telephony, and fiber optics. There is a lot of technology in an e-market, but without structure, it is useless.

The tracks define the dimensions of the transportation system: its horizons, its intersections, and its lines of communication. In B2B, the tracks are the net markets and the server-based packet transfer mechanisms of the Internet. The people who travel on the trains, or the freight that is shipped on the train, is analogous to computer data. People can be any color, any nationality; freight can be of any composition, within the constraints of the train cars. Aha! The constraints of the train cars. The train cars are the standards. People can't be too fat or they won't squeeze into the seats. Freight generally must be solid and fit in the cars; liquids and gasses must be in solid containers. The gauge of the wheels of each car must be the same as the gauge of the tracks, or else a cumbersome transfer must be made. If these standards are not respected, then the train doesn't run.

At this early stage, online marketplaces are hampered by outdated, restrictive systems and therefore are only filling specific, isolated needs. In other words, the train can get you where you want to go only if you've already told someone to pick you up and the tracks happen to head in that direction.

■ SPEAK UP. I CAN'T HEAR YOU.

Standards are the train cars that transport our ideas to others who share our standards. In the technical context of net markets, XML is emerging as the standard language. It is important to note, of course, that the human language standards used must be agreed upon as well. But we are focusing here on standards that facilitate machine-to-machine interactions.

XML allows organizations, companies, and industries to customize their own vocabulary. Using XML, electronic document formats can easily be designed to exchange business information over the Internet. In other words, XML exchanges information about information. Sound simple? It is. XML's minimalist structure offers the flexibility to be molded and customized. And its interoperability means that it can act as a translator for existing languages. This capability has led XML to be nicknamed a digital Esperanto, the

Rosetta Stone of the twenty-first century, and the lingua franca of B2B e-commerce.

But how does reducing the Tower of Babel in technology labs translate into profits for the business world? More to the point, why should a CEO care about a technological language, developed in 1996, that happens to be one of the many developments contributing to the B2B trend?

Why? Because XML is a way to sustain advantage in the face of emerging and ambitious Internet competitors. XML can make the theoretical promises of seamless e-commerce a reality. It provides the common language to create a truly universal trading community in which companies integrate their computer systems with all of their supply chain partners, regardless of industry.

In the opening speech at Comdex 2000, Bill Gates offered up his view of the state and future of the industry, and he believes XML will play a key role in that future. "Microsoft and the industry should really build their future around XML." He added, "Office 10 will feature native support for XML in the Excel spreadsheet and the Access database."

Many companies aren't waiting around for Microsoft. Visa International has already adopted XML for a new invoicing standard that will help its businesses, regardless of industry, automate their purchasing functions, as well as their travel and entertainment expenses. Traditional B2C companies Lands' End and Staples launched their B2B sites using XML to exchange data. Industry procurement specialists Ariba and Commerce One are using their own XML-based software systems to communicate among buyers and suppliers. Others are leveraging the knowledge embedded in an XML transaction to capture and maintain intelligence about supply-chain performance. Almost all software and hardware vendors have announced plans to produce XML-ready versions of their products. In addition to Microsoft and Sun, Intel has two dedicated data-center products that are designed specifically to speed XML-based data processing.

We're betting on XML, but the tool is not without its detractors—or its challenges. Its flexibility, touted as one of its greatest strengths, has also been hailed as its greatest weakness. Software companies and standards organizations across the world and the web have attempted to jump on the XML bandwagon by adding their own proprietary twist to it, thereby creating multiple flavors of XML. There is a clear danger that competing groups will define proprietary, incompatible formats that will limit XML's impact. Microsoft, for example, introduced "orchestration," an XML-based technology that essentially enables information to describe itself, with the result of faster and more accurate automated order processing. Not to be outdone, Oracle and IBM are developing their own XML-based proprietary technologies.

Another snag is that the current base of products that can accommodate XML is limited, and while XML is relatively simple, there is still only a small—albeit growing—group of skilled XML experts. Given the current crunch of today's labor market, the challenge of finding and holding on to skilled IT employees cannot be underestimated.

■ I'M TALKING. ARE YOU LISTENING?

Although this digital Esperanto is emerging, lots of companies still speak in a language that is unique to themselves and whomever it is they have traditionally talked to. Thanks to EDI, lots of retailers speak the speech of Procter & Gamble, and lots of manufacturers speak in the tongue of Wal-Mart. Hitachi speaks John Deere, and so does Bosch; but Bosch also speaks Ford. But what if you're not Ford, or Bosch, or Wal-Mart, or P&G? Then you have lots of formatting issues to deal with when you communicate with your suppliers or customers.

Only a few years ago, EDI systems were touted as the must-have e-commerce solution, and major companies across the board invested heavily in them, typically resulting in large savings of both time and money. Just as important as the cost savings already accrued, EDI systems have given many large, traditional corporations invaluable experience in participating in independent trade exchanges.

"Large manufacturers have used EDI to connect with the top 20 percent of their suppliers, which represents 80 percent of the materials they buy," says Les Wyatt, senior vice president of product marketing with Harbinger. "They have too much invested in their EDI infrastructure to change, and now that they have it working, there isn't a lot of incentive to change."

Although it is a sound, stable technology, EDI has its limitations. Remember that eight-track stereo you thought was so popular in the 1970s? That's when EDI was at its hippest as well. EDI is a custom-coded point-to-point interface, meaning that it directly ties a pair of applications or databases together. As the trading partners increase, so do the number of applications, databases, and required interfaces. Connecticut-based Gartner Group characterizes this result as "inter-application spaghetti." And EDI is labor-intensive, costly to implement and maintain, and prone to error. Redundant business logic can be encoded in multiple programs, and the engineer who wrote the specialized code may be the only one who understands it. Understandably, it seems like the first thing a company does with an EDI transaction set is change the format. There's a story about the manufacturer who got so frustrated with EDI that he said, "If we have one more successful EDI relationship, we'll go out of business."

Some industry sectors, like tobacco, never really got into EDI because the receipt confirmation process actually slowed down a less technologically advanced system of faxes and telephone calls. EDI is clunky and eclectic, great for some things, but ultimately not scalable—just like a lot of the technology of the era of the 1970s that spawned it. It works great (well, okay) for the Procter and Wal-Mart or Bosch and Ford dialogs, but it doesn't do as well for small-

and medium-sized enterprises, which greatly limits the pool of electronically linked trading partners.

XML-based systems, on the other hand, open the door to the world of information exchange. And compared to EDI, XML's cost of implementation is low, and its open, flexible standards encourage more participation from more industries. XML-based systems can include sweeping information descriptions that are not limited to the transaction. And, because it is compatible with Internet messaging protocols, XML documents can be securely transmitted over the Internet without modifications to firewalls.

Although the future of e-commerce will be built upon XML, the next several years of transition will see both XML and EDI coexisting peacefully. Luckily, translation of EDI into XML and XML into EDI is straightforward. XML's flexibility means that it is not an either-or technology; companies can continue to use their EDI systems and even enhance them with XML to create universal trading communities.

Nothing the net markets are doing requires that participants eliminate all of their EDI relationships, but most participants will want to eliminate them eventually in order to enjoy the benefit that the net markets are going to bring them.

■ MAY I HAVE THIS DANCE?

The rules of a net market are a lot like dance steps; you really can't fox-trot unless your partner knows how and is willing. The rapid growth of trade exchanges has left companies dancing with a slew of different partners from different industries, each with its unique take on the fox-trot.

What happens when every industry dances to its own steps, or, more aptly, has its own rules to define data standards? In North America, most industries use the 11-digit UPC to identify products. In Europe and Asia Pacific, companies hold fast to a 12-digit EAN (European Article Number) product number that is used on products in nearly 100 countries. These are two diverse systems that require different labels and different protocols for updating prices. The trouble is, two standards are one too many in a global economy. Just as on the dance floor, two can tango, but only one can lead. In the WWRE, for example, member companies either use the UPC or the EAN. So a price change performed at the cash register with one system will not affect a price change in products coded under the other system. Confusion threatens.

Adding to the confusion, identification numbers between supply-chain partners frequently change or aggregate as the item moves down the supply chain from manufacturer to distributor to reseller. Companies are left to sort out product numbering issues by hand or with custom programming. Buyers are in a worse spot. As more people turn to Internet shopping for speed and convenience, they run into bottlenecks caused by the same identification numbers for different products and parts.

Recognizing the problem, last year, the Uniform Code Council and EAN International joined forces to create a global standard for unique product identification. Called the global trade item number (GTIN), this 14-digit number encompasses both the UPC and the EAN symbols on retail products. GTIN is designed to ease worldwide communication and e-commerce processes, including full tracking and tracing of inventories, orders, billing, and transportation. There will be less confusion, fewer errors, and not as many returns. Fortunately, companies will not—repeat *not*—have to reengineer their databases to accommodate the new identification standard. RosettaNet has created a way to map existing product numbering systems to the GTIN standard.

The ability to identify locations is another prerequisite to successful electronic trading. All organizations exchange information, both externally and internally, and while it is assumed that the information exchange occurs between the right parties, in many instances there is no way to guarantee it. Here global location numbers (GLNs) can help. Presented in bar-code format, GLNs provide a unique, unambiguous, and efficient means of communicating precise names and locations. With GLNs, names, addresses, and information about particular locations do not need to be communicated for every transaction. Instead, the necessary information is entered only once into computer files and is retrieved by referring to a unique, standard location number.

Global trade item numbers and global location numbers are proving to be the answer for organizations that are struggling to sort out the challenges of standardization.

■ AHEAD OF THE CURVE

Some industry sectors are way ahead of the curve on data standards, and others haven't even really started. In general, providers of things that rarely change or that are highly engineered, sequenced, or programmed, have agreed on how to describe the characteristics of their products. Providers of fashion or of seasonal, perishable, or service-content products have found it more difficult to settle on standards for how to describe their products.

UCCnet, a universal foundation for electronic commerce spanning all industries and geographies, is on the leading edge of the curve. UCCnet offers its participants an open, standards-based Internet trading community. In time, it will provide a universal infrastructure of compliant data regardless of how companies identify their products. So whatever identification system a company uses, whether universal product codes or universal product numbers or any other universal article number, the numbers can be loaded into the UCCnet system. UCCnet guarantees that the exchange of that data is both compliant and can be accessed in real time.

RosettaNet is a nonprofit organization that is developing XML standards for data exchange within the technology supply chain—connecting component manufacturers, distributors, resellers, and purchasers. Its goal is to eliminate the need for customized interfaces. The RosettaNet standards include not only the XML documents, but also the implementation framework (exchange protocols) and the partner dialog and processes supporting the required interactions. Rosetta Net's membership list is impressive—it includes Cisco, FedEx, GE Information Services, Hewlett-Packard, and Toshiba.

GCI (Global Commerce Initiative) is a joint effort of 40 of the world's leading manufacturers and retailers working together to create the first global standards for Internet trading in the consumer goods industry. So far, GCI has sponsored two global pilot projects. The first tests the transmission of simple business-to-business transaction among global companies, such as sending a purchase order over the Internet. The trading partners are Royal Ahold, one of the world's largest food providers and a founding member of WWRE, and Johnson & Johnson, a worldwide manufacturer of healthcare and consumer products. The pilot will take place across countries including the United States, Argentina, and the Netherlands. The second pilot tests the functionality of trade exchanges over the Internet and includes Procter & Gamble, Metro AG, UCCnet, and Transora.

GCI is also working on setting standards for things like collaborative planning, forecasting, and replenishment. But some people think that this takes GCI out of the train car business and expands its footprint to include the tracks— and the executives of the big and successful companies worry that their competitive advantage may be dissipated. They've learned to dance well, and they're not going to let a bunch of bureaucrats change the way they cut the rug.

Outside of these industry-specific efforts, no single standard nor standards organization has emerged as the front-runner—and one is not expected for several years. So, here we are, talking about technology and about standards. And that leads to the ultimate question: What does the future of e-markets look like? In Chapter 13, we'll dust off that crystal ball.

■ QUESTIONS

How broadly are EDI relationships implemented throughout your organization? Are they primarily used in large and well-developed supplier/customer relationships, or are they broadly available to small and medium-sized partners?

How much do you modify standard EDI transaction sets? Is maintenance a big issue—that is, one that might provide an incentive to exploit XML technologies more quickly?

How are UPC/EAN codes used in your business? Does your company adhere to the letter or the spirit of the standards? (For example, do you always get a new UPC when package characteristics change?) What is the share of proprietary versus standard formats for your transaction sets?

How involved are you in your industry sector's standard-setting activity? Why aren't you more involved?

13
Chapter

What Happens Next?

It's become axiomatic to assert that XYZ technology enhancement or business process improvement will change everything. Of course it will. That's what this book is all about. Just as Henry Ford could never have imagined that the car would lead to creation of the suburbs, trying to read the crystal ball 10 years or more out is murky at best. But you know it won't stop us from trying . . . we're consultants.

The broad launch and implementation of net markets, particularly those led by industry Power Players, promises to fundamentally transform the economic model of business in the future. It will take a decade—at least—to effect this transformation. When it is done, every aspect of business will be altered: the way people work, the way product moves, the way warehouses are built, the way offices are laid out (and even whether people work in offices), and the way sector profits are divided up among players. How big is this change? The industrial revolution and the agricultural revolution are the only analogous antecedents.

This book has focused on what is happening now, and the abyss between the way things work now and what will be required in the future to exploit net markets and Internet exchanges. Sometimes the changes seem insurmountable, and sometimes the investment is hard for corporations to justify—it may seem like the change that will take a transaction cost from $10 down to $1 costs $11!

But we know that electricity went from an uneconomic oddity (like the Internet in the 1960s and 1970s) to the key enabling technology for business: motive power, communications, office design, logistics—everything changes. So what is the future of the Power Players' net markets? What will the future hold 10, 20 years ahead? What should leading companies be thinking now about concrete things like infrastructure, as well as human capital things such as training and recruiting, so that their competency and skills portfolios migrate to what will be needed in the future?

It is clear that the net market revolution is currently in its clunky-technology phase. Simple things are difficult, and complex things are nearly impossible. Four transformations will take place before the dawn of the new era truly lights up the sky:

➤ *Combing the magic throughout the value chain.* It just takes time, but there's something in it for everybody.

➤ *Agreeing on how to talk to each other.* We need standards: for data, for sharing it, and for using it.

➤ *Burying the successful legacies of the past.* Systems and the ways of using systems must change.

➤ *Moving the people out of the way.* Finding ways to let your things talk to other people's things.

■ COMBING THE MAGIC THROUGH THE VALUE CHAIN

Everyone knows there's tremendous power in the Internet, but at this point even the most prescient cannot fathom the extent, range, and impact that these technologies will have. A good analog is the implementation of bar codes in common use today throughout the consumer marketplace. When introduced in 1973, many companies thought bar codes would be good for some products but not for all. Now they are ubiquitous. Where once executives envisioned bar codes as a way to eliminate price stickers and the practice of hand stamping prices on cans, they failed to grasp the extent of the value that product bar codes would provide up and down the value chain. What far-sighted visionary saw those little bar code lines and thought of ways to streamline and rethink supply-chain tracking, inventory planning, category management, planogramming, promotion management, and measurement? The list of affected areas goes on and on. And the benefits associated with the implementation of this very straightforward and easily implemented technology far surpassed even the most ambitious of expectations. But the amount of time it took to comb the magic through the value chain was a lot longer than anyone would have predicted, too. How long should it take to slap a bar code or two on your packaging? Well, most players will tell you it took at least 10 years to play the whole thing out—from the initial planning stage until the benefits were effectively wrung out of the value chain.

Now, how much more sophisticated than bar coding is the Internet technology on which the net markets rest? How much more complex and far-reaching are the paths and cascades of value flowing through the relationships among partners? How much more elemental—and, therefore, fundamentally transforming—is the nature of the technology? If product bar coding were akin to providing your house with an electronic address plate, a fully implemented Internet technology would require replacing every nail, screw, and bolt in your house with its e-counterpart.

Certainly, much of the work will have been done in the next 10 years, but we should anticipate that industry sector transformation will continue for 30 to 40 years to come.

■ AGREEING ON COMMUNICATION METHODS

Industry transformation can move forward a lot easier if everybody agrees on how to talk to one other. The development of the DVD sector, based on an agreement among the key players, enjoyed much more rapid development than the hit-and-miss development of the mag tape sector with its multiple formats of reel-to-reel, eight-track, and cassettes struggling against each other and the equipment marketplace.

In the rarified realm of data and information, agreement on standards is even more powerful. But there are two obstacles to widespread acceptance. The first is settling on agreed-upon standards; the second in executing those agreements.

Agreeing on standards is always difficult because by definition it requires someone to change from whatever it is they are currently doing—if no change were required then standards would be de facto already in existence. Further, some players think that their unique approach to data gives them a competitive advantage—and in an imperfect world, it may (although that competitive advantage may evaporate in the face of a reset of the playing rules). In the current environment, it is clear that agreeing on communication standards (like XML) is clearly in the interest of all players, and agreeing on data-field standards is probably in the interest of all players as well. In a benevolent dictatorship, standards would be dictated and we would be done with it and happy we would be. In an open market environment, each sector is a Pushmi-Pullyu with the Power Players trying to apply body English to the resulting standards.

In an evolutionary sense, however, standards will be set, and nonconforming players will be marginalized. Agreeing on standards at the outset speeds up the process, but it doesn't substantially change the outcome.

Of far more import is the reality of how difficult it is to execute and syndicate the agreement on standards: hundreds of thousands of companies, millions of SKUs, hundreds of data elements. Very quickly you can envision a Flemish tapestry with a quintillion stitches: easy in concept, damned difficult in reality.

What will the future hold? Well, you can be pretty sure Procter & Gamble and Wal-Mart will find agreement in their communications, but what of P&G's one thousand smallest customers and a thousand of Wal-Mart's smallest suppliers? And you can safely place a bet that Cincinnati and Bentonville will see eye to eye, but what of Milano or Montevideo?

The Pareto rule will continue to apply as well: Communication about the 20 percent of the SKUs that account for 80 percent of the business will get standardized quickly. This creates an opportunity for data intermediaries and third-party service providers to provide utility services to this segment to allow them to participate in net market activities.

■ BURYING THE SUCCESSFUL LEGACIES OF THE PAST

Successful companies are constantly taking make-buy decisions to figure out what they do themselves and what they let others do. Often these decisions rest on what these companies think provide them with a unique competitive advantage. But technological changes frequently have thrown these decisions into upheaval. Ford Motor Company used to raise sheep for the woolen roof liners of their vehicles, now Jacques Nasser has pondered aloud whether they really should be in the business of building cars.

The technological changes inherent in net markets are so far-reaching that we could anticipate sweeping changes in what companies do themselves and what they let others do. And so it will happen. But what does the industry do with the billions of dollars worth of computers, warehouses, offices, and equipment that will be rendered superfluous by net market technology? Like all similar techno-shifts in the past, these resources will be reallocated to other parts of the economy. What's the big deal? Well, the difference with net markets is that, unlike the more-than-a-century it took electricity to go from nowhere to everywhere, a substantial amount of the evolution in net markets will play out over the next 5 to 10 years.

This means that in addition to developing new capabilities and skills, and investing in new resources and assets, companies that will be most successful in exploiting net market technologies also have to be most successful at modifying or shutting down their legacy IT systems, reshaping office environments, retraining their people, and recalibrating their supply-chain resources. There are two ingredients necessary to succeed: a good strategy for growth and the ability to eliminate frictional barriers to growth. In the fast-paced net market environment, the second may be the more important. As one CEO remarked, "I'm going to shoot the next person who comes up with a good idea. I have too many good ideas already. What I really need is execution."

■ LEAD, FOLLOW, OR GET OUT OF THE WAY

Right now, everyone talks about how wonderful the Internet is because, like the better mousetrap, it brings the world to our doorsteps. For businesses, net markets are exciting because we can get everything, from anywhere, all the time.

But businesses are still run by people, and people hit overload pretty quickly. Successful net market implementation will mean getting the human filter out of the way of the data. That means getting the decision rules out of people's heads and into the net markets' logic structure. This isn't easy and has little to do with technology. But that's what is needed to get to the next stage of development, which is T2T communication. T2T is where my bot talks to your bot and they make decisions based on what we've told them. If they can't, unlike *2001*'s HAL, they don't self-destruct, but rather, escalate the interaction back to their human. The conversations between the T's may not be worthy of a sequel to *My Dinner With Andre,* but they may be more complex than many people realize.

Consider, for example, that some of our favorite gadgets and appliances are already well engrossed in conversations with each other. Many of today's cell phones are Internet enabled, meaning that you can not only send and receive e-mail messages, you can also use them to buy virtually anything and everything off the Internet—including that autographed Joe DiMaggio baseball card you found on eBay. In fact, eBay will even automatically notify you through your phone if somebody else places a higher bid. Courtesy of a brief exchange between your cell phone and eBay's server, Joltin' Joe will be yours.

Remember all of the legal wrangling that the music site Napster went through in 2000 and 2001? Whether your sympathy rested with Metallica and the record industry or the kid in the dorm trying to swipe some free tunes, the real headline of the story rests with the technology that enabled all of the music swapping. Peer-to-peer (P2P) communication allows computers to speak directly to one another, trading files—including MP3s—without a server acting as an intermediary. That's what allowed Napster, for example, never to store copyrighted material; it simply connected users directly to the music files of other users—one computer talking directly to another.

Beyond the ongoing commentary on MTV, the ramifications for this technology in the business world are significant: If and when IT departments adopt P2P, it will change (yet again) the way companies collaborate with one another—possibly eliminating the need for intermediaries such as net markets altogether. Just as Napster was a utility, not a record collection, so the value of this technology is in the connections, not the content.

In the future, then, humans will be able to focus on fewer, more relevant issues. Their decisions on those tougher issues can then be crafted into rules that will increase the sophistication of the bot's decision-making capability.

Brave new world? Scary future? Not really. We've been doing this for centuries already with *people* as our bots. Think about it. If anything, the increased productivity coming from this development will allow humans to do more human things and fewer systematic, low-discretion things, and as a result, the quality of human life will increase. Will machines be able to think like humans, with the same sophistication and nuance? Probably not, but who cares? We already have machines that think like people—people! And we seem to have gotten a good system down pat for making more of them. The challenge for developed-world companies is to extend the productivity-enhancing effects of the Internet and net markets to our colleagues and customers in Africa, South America, and South Asia.

The development of net markets is in its essence a democratizing force in business. It increases productivity and increases the quality of human life. It breaks down the command-and-control hierarchy of the traditional business structure, and it fosters a more collaborative trading community within companies and across enterprises.

So what does the future look like in 50 years? Humans still exist and they are still in control of machines. But machines are more evenly distributed throughout human life. Preset decision rules will be embedded in cars, refrigerators, lift-trucks, pallets, packages, and paint cans. The flow of information—and its modification and use—will be largely transparent to the humans it serves. We'll still make decisions to solve problems and set new decision rules.

Two challenges threaten this bright future. First, because humans get to choose what to do with information, they can choose to do bad things with it as well as good things.

This book describes the many positive things that increased flow and velocity of information bring to the business world, but privacy violations and security breaches are equally plausible scenarios. Increased technology gives us increased choice, but like Adam and Eve in the garden, it also requires us to choose carefully. Second, we must be careful to educate and train people throughout the economy, lest an upper class of techno-literates refuses to share resources with a brutish, snarling underclass of technology have-nots, with few expectations and substantially lower per capita incomes.

Wayne Gretzky, perhaps the best Power Player of them all on the ice, is famously quoted as saying, "I don't skate to where the puck is, I skate to where it's going to be." The same holds true for the Power Players in the business world: If the Power Players can successfully address these challenges and can focus on the aspects of net markets that enhance productivity and improve quality of life, then their initiatives in net markets in the early years of the 2000s will create a foundation for a robust and enriched future. We believe the Power Players are more than ready for the tasks that lie ahead.

Part

Toolbox

We're consultants, so we wouldn't meet your expectations if we didn't leave you with multiple lists and collections of things to think about. After all, the whole genesis of this book was our desire to pass along to you the knowledge we have picked up from our clients and learned while working with them on some of the groundbreaking B2B markets that are making headlines—and changing the way business is done.

Back in the Introduction, we said that the rules of B2B markets have changed and are changing still. Certainly, the editors of this book have rewritten whole sections, not only because once-promising sites have hit the skids while this book was under development but because we have developed whole new theories about the future of e-markets while we talked to the experts who helped us craft the contents.

We are well aware that, in the time before you pick up this book to read it, more change will happen. For any inconsistencies or inaccuracies that may result due to time-liness, we apologize. For all updates, visit us at < www. atkearney.com >. We'll try to keep the material in this book fresh in an online medium.

In the next pages, we've included a glossary of e-terms, a list of our favorite web sites, and a list of the members to the B2B markets discussed in-depth in Part III. We hope these lists will help to keep the B2B marketplace in perspective.

Glossary

It's a brave new world of electronic marketing, complete with its own fashion apparel (the basic black e-suit), cool accoutrements (PDAs and cells) and verbiage. Jargon is useful, enjoyable, and necessary. One of our favorite pastimes is asking what acronyms mean and savoring the first five or six best guesses. Here's a list of current terms and generally accepted definitions.

ASP Format. Active server page—a web page that uses ActiveX scripting, usually VB Script or Jscript code.

ASPs. Application service providers—third-party information technology providers that distribute and manage software services and solutions.

ATM. Asynchronous transfer mode—technology that transfers information in small cells, which enables efficient transmission of video, audio, and computer data over the same network.

Automated Proxy Bidding. Complex contingencies built into the overall purchase of products, enabling bidders to buy on the terms they need.

B2B. Business-to-business, such as < WWRE.org >.

B2C. Business-to-consumer, such as < JCREW.com >.

B2E. Business-to-employee, such as a proprietary human resources system.

Bandwidth. A measure of the quantity of information that can be transmitted over a network in a specific period of time.

Binary Code. Number system made up of 0s and 1s, used for executable programs and numeric data.

Bot. Abbreviation of robot.

Broadband. High-speed transmission that permits simultaneous transmission of video, voice, and data.

Bundling and Unbundling Capability. Option to buy goods either together or separately, allowing bidders to obtain the best price for their combination of items.

C2C. Consumer-to-consumer, such as eBay.

Catalog. E-market aggregation of the offerings of more than one vendor into a one-stop-shop that facilitates product comparisons, customized presentations, and more rapid identification of preferred goods.

CGI. Common gateway interface—defines how a web server communicates with other software within the same computer.

Coalition Approach. Bringing together an entire network of peers to establish an e-marketplace and structuring the network in such a way that all members are able to generate value and create a profit.

Commerce. The business model used by the net market to make money. It can include auctions, catalogs, or a liquid exchange.

Connectivity. This can mean connecting participants to the site, establishing connections across the entire supply chain, and connecting with other exchanges.

Content. The relevant information included on the site, including text, images, sound, data, video, and graphics.

CPFR. Collaboration, planning, forecasting, and replenishment.

Data Mining. Using a database to find patterns among data. Commonly used by companies to find common demographics and customer preferences.

Data Warehousing. Combining different databases that have a wide variety of information to get an overall picture of business conditions.

Diachronic Information. Information across time. Measures inventory as it passes through the value chain. (See also Synchronic or Stock Information.)

Direct Goods. Items that are primary to the production process.

E2E. Exchange-to-exchange.

EAN. European Article Numbering—code format, similar to UPC, widely used in Europe and Asia.

ECR. Efficient consumer response.

EDI. Electronic data interchange.

E-Procurement. Paperless purchasing and payment processes via online catalogs or operating databases.

ERP. Enterprise resource planning.

Extraconnection. Connection of one group of value-chain partners in one net market to another group of value-chain partners in another net market.

Fiber-Optic. Cables that use glass or plastic threads to transmit data on lightwaves.

Firewall. Network security system that prevents access by unauthorized users.

First-Mover Advantage. Business gains achieved by being earliest to harness technology or provide a service or offering.

Forward Auction. Auction with one seller and many buyers.

Frame Agreement. Contract that serves multiple companies to achieve the economies of scale needed to allow suppliers to cut costs from their supply chain.

GCI. Global Commerce Initiative—joint effort of 40 leading manufacturers and retailers to create global standards for e-trading in the consumer goods industry.

GLN. Global location number—presented in bar-code format, they provide a unique, efficient means of communicating precise names and locations.

GTIN. Global trade item number—14-digit number that encompasses both the UPC and EAN symbols on retail products.

Horizontal Exchanges. Cross-industry net markets that help buyers reduce the purchase price of goods and services through a more competitive supplier base, greater buying power, and spot-buy opportunities.

Hyperauction. Auction that uses defined standardized buying criteria to enable automated complex transactions.

Indirect Goods. Items such as office supplies that are necessary to run a business but are not directly involved with the production process.

Industry-Sponsored Market. Consortium of industry players that typically have control over some combination of product, distribution, customers, and suppliers.

Interconnection. Connection among value-chain participants involved in a transaction.

Intraconnection. Connection of internal processes within the buyer and seller organizations.

Legacy Systems. A corporation's existing IT systems that may or may not have the bandwidth and capability to carry today's traffic seamlessly and with transparency.

Liquid Exchange. Nasdaq-like exchange that allows multiple buyers and sellers to trade in real time with all requests filled automatically using transparent prices.

Liquidity. Volume of transactions conducted in the net market.

Many to Many. The concept behind net markets, in which many buyers have access to many sellers (and vice versa).

M-Commerce. Mobile commerce.

Multiparameter Bidding. Standard buying parameters such as quality rating, technical specifications, or brand name that enable participants to concentrate on variables other than price.

P2P. Peer-to-peer.

Pareto Rule. Also known as the 80/20 rule, it states that 80 percent of the benefit comes from 20 percent of the costs; or, 80 percent of anything is related to 20 percent of something else.

Plug-and-Play. Capability that gives users the ability to plug a device into a computer and have the computer automatically recognize that the device is there.

Proprietary Net Markets. E-markets that run by rules that tend to favor the founders or select members.

Pure-Play Net Markets. Neutral and typically nimble e-markets that appeal to a wide base of buyers and suppliers. They appear particularly in fragmented industries with no power base on either the buying or selling side.

Relationship Intermediaries. Online agents connecting buyers and sellers in fragmented markets to provide critical industry information or potential cost savings.

Reverse Auction. Auction with one buyer and many sellers.

SCM. Supply chain management—the process of optimizing the delivery of goods, services, and information from supplier to customer.

Single Contract. Agreement that serves multiple companies to achieve the economies of scale needed to allow suppliers to cut costs from their supply chain.

Stickiness. Eagerness of users to return to a specific Internet site.

Subscription Fee. Annual fee for all members of an e-market.

Synchronic or Stock Information. Information at a point in time. Measures inventory as it sits at points along the value chain. (See also Diachronic Information.)

T2T. Thing-to-thing.

Transactional Intermediaries. Agents focused on simplifying purchase orders, invoicing, and payment processes. Takes place primarily between sellers of complementary products and a fragmented customer base.

UPC. Universal Product Code—bar-code system adopted by the U.S. grocery industry in the 1970s.

Vertical Distributors. Agents that pull together a diverse group of companies, automate their transactions, and manage the flow of goods and services.

Vertical Exchanges. Industry-specific net markets that offer better prices and lower transaction costs with the ultimate goal of improving supply-chain performance.

VICS. Voluntary Interindustry Commerce Standards—develops CPFR guidelines.

XML. Extensible markup language—emerging as the standard language for e-business transmission of data sets.

Web Sites

Everyone has their favorite web sites, just as everyone has their favorite search engine. Here is a collection of the e-market-places mentioned in this book, a few more of our favorites, and the most popular ones. Be warned: This list is up-to-date as of press time but subject to change with or without notice. For updates, check our own web site: <www.atkearney.com>! We'll also host a URL farm with these sites to facilitate your exploration.

➤ <www.58K.com>: Reverse auction for printing jobs
➤ <www.aceva.com>: An e-finance infrastructure provider
➤ <www.adauction.com>: Media e-marketplace
➤ <www.aerospan.com>: Comprehensive e-market-place for the global air transportation industry
➤ <www.aeroxchange.com>: Coalition e-marketplace serving the airline industry
➤ <www.ahold.com>: Rapidly growing international food provider with a presence in net markets
➤ <www.aice.com>: (American IC Exchange) Exchange of commodity semiconductors and computer products
➤ <www.airnewco>: Supply-chain exchange for leading airlines
➤ <www.alibaba.com>: Import/export trade site
➤ <www.altra.com>: energy e-marketplace
➤ <www.amazon.com>: Online seller of books, music and other items
➤ <www.ariba.com>: B2B commerce platform
➤ <www.arzoon.com>: Developer of enterprise-class supply-chain software primarily for logistics and transportation

➤ < www.assetsb2b.com >: Hong Kong–based auctioneer of used and idle assets for Asian Pacific and North American markets

➤ < www.autodaq >: Forward auction that facilitates the trade of wholesale cars on the Internet

➤ < www.autoparts.com >: Automotive e-marketplace

➤ < www.biobid.com >: Online marketplace for high-end pre-owned biotechnology and pharmaceutical capital assets

➤ < www.bluelight.com >: Kmart's e-commerce site

➤ < www.capclear.com >: Virtual clearinghouse

➤ < www.celarix.com >: Provider of webcentric collaborative technology to improve global supply chain

➤ < www.chemconnect.com >: B2B trading marketplace and information portal for worldwide chemicals, plastics, and industrial gas buyers and sellers

➤ < www.cisco.com >: Network-equipment maker

➤ < www.clareon.com >: Online provider of business payment solutions

➤ < www.commerceone.com >: E-commerce applications provider

➤ < www.comps.com >: Commercial property catalog that helps match buyers and sellers but leaves prices to be determined in offline negotiations

➤ < www.converge.com >: Net marketplace (formerly eHITEX) formed by an HP-led coalition of companies, centered around the common supplier base of the computer, telecom equipment, and consumer electronics industries

➤ < www.covisint.com >: Automotive e-business trading exchange, supported by General Motors, Ford, and DaimlerChrysler, joined by Renault/Nissan

➤ < www.creditex.com >: Online financial services platform to facilitate liquidity, standardization, and transparency in credit derivatives

➤ < www.datastream.net >: Asset maintenance management e-commerce site

➤ < www.dovebid.com >: Capital-assets and valuation services company offering both Webcast and online capital asset auctions, as well as an array of value-added B2B services

➤ < www.e2open.com >: Net marketplace centered around the common supplier base of the computer, telecom equipment, and consumer electronics industries

➤ < www.ebay.com >: C2C auction site

➤ < www.ebreviate.com >: An EDS company providing eSourcing solutions for B2B buying, including Internet Negotiations, RFPs, Sourcing Surveys, and Sourcing Management Technologies

➤ < www.esteel.com >: Steel e-marketplace

➤ < www.e-zine.com >: List of electronic magazines around the world. No longer updated

➤ < www.foodtrader.com >: e-marketplace for ingredient suppliers to consumer goods manufacturers

➤ < www.foodusa.com >: Liquid exchange for agribusiness

➤ < www.globalfoodexchange.com >: Provider of web-based software that enables retailers, wholesalers, foodservice distributors, manufacturers, and suppliers to manage the sourcing, procurement, and transport of perishable and non-perishable products

➤ < www.globalsources.com >: End-to-end e-commerce solution supporting the day-to-day business operations of international trading partners

➤ < www.gnx.com >: Globally integrated retail supply-chain network

➤ < www.gofish.com >: Liquid exchange for fish

➤ < www.houstonstreet.com: E-marketplace for energy trading

➤ < www.i2.com >: B2B solution that incorporates a complete supply-chain model, marketplace-to-marketplace support, and content-management capabilities

➤ < www.iprocure.com >: MRO procurement web site (this link directs you to the Datastream web site)

➤ < www.jcpenny.com >: Retail store with strong online presence

➤ < www.kingfisher.com >: U.K.-based consumer electronics, home improvement, and general merchandise company, also a member of WWRE

➤ < www.marketmile.com >: B2B e-commerce company serving mid-sized businesses' purchasing of everyday business products and services using an e-procurement application and marketplace

➤ < www.meetchina.com >: China's leading trade portal for businesses worldwide to source and procure products directly from China

➤ < www.menerva.com >: Software provider for e-marketplace infrastructure

➤ < www.metalsite.com >: Metals exchange and industry information provider

➤ < www.metaltradenet.com >: E-marketplace for trading steel in Europe

➤ < www.metreo.com >: E-business software provider

➤ < www.monster.com >: Online job hunting web site

➤ < www.myaircraft.com >: Decision-support and commerce services for aerospace industry supply-chain partners

➤ < www.myfacility.com >: Exchange soon to be launched by Honeywell

➤ < www.necx.com >: High-tech and electronic e-marketplace

➤ < www.netbuy.com >: Online, multivendor catalog for electronic components

➤ < www.novopoint.com >: Coalition e-marketplace in the food-and-beverage industry

➤ < www.oracle.com >: One of the world's largest software companies

➤ < www.paper2print.com >: B2B e-commerce portal, designed to increase the efficiency and effectiveness of all participants in the printing-paper industry supply chain

➤ < www.paperexchange.com > : Global e-business marketplace for the pulp and paper industry

➤ < www.partminer.com > : Provider of online business-to-business procurement services for the electronic components industry

➤ < www.partsbase.com > : online seller of parts for the aviation, aerospace, and defense industries.

➤ < www.peapod.com > : Online grocery store

➤ < www.pcorder.com > : E-commerce solutions that enable the computer industry's suppliers, resellers, and end users to buy and sell computer products online

➤ < www.redknife.com > : Provider of a range of functionality to enable commerce and collaboration with a trading community; services include data warehousing, vendor enablement, order management, and 24/7 active monitoring

➤ < www.rosettanet.org > : a consortium of computer makers, resellers, and users creating e-commerce standards for transaction-center data exchanges using a standardized set of terms for product, partner, and transaction properties

➤ < www.sabre.com > : Provider of IT solutions for travel and transportation industry

➤ < www.sap.com > : Provider of interenterprise software

➤ < www.seebeyond.com > : Provider of e-business integration solutions

➤ < www.seguer.com > : Asset inventory services provider

➤ < www.semiconbay.com > : Provider of B2B, auction, and exchange services for the semiconductor industry

➤ < www.telecentric.com > : Provider of integrated e-business solutions, from network design through deployment, to the telecom industry

➤ < www.tesco.com > : Online grocery delivery service

➤ < www.tires.com > : E-marketplace for tires

➤ < www.tradenetone.com > : Logistics e-marketplace

➤ < www.tradeout.com > : Online marketplace for businesses buying and selling excess inventory and idle assets

➤ < www.tradepayment.com > : Developer of e-commerce technologies that automate net markets

➤ < www.transora.com > : Net marketplace for the food, beverage, and consumer products industries

➤ < www.uccnet.org > : An open, standards-based, scaleable, distributed Internet trading community that is industry supported and sponsored

➤ < www.ventro.com > : Provider of products and services that help online B2B marketplaces through the various stages of development

➤ < www.verticalnet.com > : E-commerce enabler focused on building and managing dynamic industry communities that provide online information resources, communication vehicles, and e-commerce channels in industrial, professional, and technology-based sectors

➤ < www.works.com > : E-marketplace for indirect goods (formerly < www.orderzone.com >)

➤ < www.webmethods.com > : Provider of integration software solutions

➤ < www.worldoffruit > : Liquid exchange for fruit

➤ < www.worldspan.com > : Provider of worldwide electronic distribution of travel information, Internet products and connectivity, and e-commerce capabilities for travel agencies

➤ < www.worldwideretailexchange.org > : Global B2B exchange enabling retailers and suppliers to substantially reduce costs across product development, e-procurement, and supply-chain processes

➤ < www.b2b.yahoo.com > : Yahoo! B2B marketplace

E-Market
Membership Lists

Remember how we said that the Power Player B2B markets are big? What we really meant is that they are BIG! Like the proverbial photo that is worth a thousand words, the following membership lists—up-to-date as of press time—provide a clear picture of the clout of the markets discussed in detail in Part III.

■ WORLDWIDE RETAIL EXCHANGE MEMBERS

➤ United States

< www.albertsons.com >
< www.bestbuy.com >
< www.cvs.com >
< www.gap.com >
< www.jcpenney.com >
< www.kmart.com >
< www.longs.com >
< www.meijer.com >
< www.publix.com >
< www.radioshack.com >
< www.riteaid.com >
< www.safeway.com >
< www.supervalu.com >
< www.target.com >
< www.walgreens.com >
< www.wegmans.com >
< www.winn-dixie.com >

➤ Europe

< www.ahold.com >
< www.auchan.com >
< www.boots.co.uk >
< www.casino.fr >
< www.cora-auto.fr >
< www.delhaize-le-lion.be >
< www.dixons-group-plc.co.uk >
< www.dsg.dk >
< www.edeka.de >
< www.elcorteingles.es >
< www.galerieslafayette.com >
< www.john-lewis.co.uk >
< www.kesko.se >
< www.kingfisher.com >
< www.marksandspencer.com >
< www.otto-group.com >
< www.safeway.co.uk >
< www.schlecker.com >
< www.tesco.com >

➤ Asia and Africa

< www.dairyfarmgroup.com >
< www.jusco.co.jp >
< www.seibu.co.jp >
< www.wooltru.co.za >
< www.woolworths.com.au >

■ COVISINT

➤ OEMs

United States

< www.daimlerchrysler.com >

< www.ford.com >

< www.gm.com >

Europe

< www.renault.com >

Asia

< www.nissandriven.com >

➤ Technology Partners

United States

< www.commerceone.com >

< www.oracle.com >

➤ Business Partners

United States

< www.aksteel.com >

< www.arvinmeritor.com >

< www.bwauto.com >

< www.collinsaikman.com >

< www.dana.com >

< www.delphiauto.com >

< www.denso.co.jp >

< www.duraauto.com >

< www.federal-mogul.com >

< www.freudenberg-nok.com >

< www.johnsoncontrols.com >

< www.lear.com >

< www.magnaint.com >

< www.towerautomotive.com >

< www.visteon.com >

< www.yazaki-group.com >

Europe

< www.autoliv.com >

< www.basf.com >

Index